HOLOCAUST AFTERMATH: CONTINUING IMPACT ON THE GENERATIONS

A Special Issue of
The Journal of Psychology and Judaism

Edited By
REUVEN P. BULKA, PH.D.

HUMAN SCIENCES PRESS, INC.
72 Fifth Avenue   3 Henrietta Street
NEW YORK, NY 10011 ● LONDON, WC2E 8LU

HUMAN SCIENCES PRESS
72 Fifth Avenue
New York, NY 10011

Printed in the United States of America

Library of Congress Catalog Number 81-84341
ISBN: 0-89885-127-0
Copyright 1981 by Human Sciences Press

JOURNAL OF
psychology
AND
judaism

Volume 6, Number 1, Fall/Winter 1981

THE JOURNAL OF PSYCHOLOGY AND JUDAISM is dedicated to exploring the relationship between psychology and Judaism and examines this relationship on both a clinical and philosophical level. The *Journal* publishes articles that are related to the spheres of psychology and Judaism and have implications concerning the synthesis of the two areas. The *Journal* serves as a forum for discussion and development of integrated approaches to uniquely Jewish problems in the clinical and meta-clinical realm. MANUSCRIPTS should be submitted in triplicate to the Editor, Dr. Reuven J. Bulka, *Journal of Psychology and Judaism*, 1747 Featherston Drive, Ottawa, Ontario, Canada, K1H 6P4. Manuscripts should be typed on one side of the page; double-spaced throughout, on 8½" x 11" paper. A margin of at least one inch should be left on all sides. A title page should contain the names of all authors and sufficient addresses. A biography of 50-75 words should be included, (academic degrees, professional interests, publications), along with a full face photograph. An abstract of no more than 100 words should accompany the manuscript. References should be listed following the style used by the American Psychological Association Publication Manual, 2nd ed. (1974). Citations from the *Bible, Talmud, Midrash, Maimonides, Shulchan Arukh*, etc., should be incorporated into the text in parentheses following the pertinent quote or statement. The reference should refer to the overall work, not the specific volume. Where possible, references should identify standard English translations of the aforementioned works. Further information concerning the preparation of manuscripts can be obtained from the Editor. Articles and books for review should be mailed to The Critical Review, 3379 Berkeley Road, Cleveland, OH 44118.

SUBSCRIPTIONS are on an academic year basis; $14.00 per year. Institutional rates are $28. Prices slightly higher outside the United States. ADVERTISING and subscription inquiries should be made to: Human Sciences Press, 72 Fifth Avenue, N.Y., N.Y. 10011, (212) 243-6000.

INDEXED in: Psychological Abstracts, Index to Jewish Periodicals, Current Contents/Social and Behavioral Sciences, Religious and Theological Abstracts, Social Sciences Citation Index, Selected Lists of Tables of Contents of Psychiatric Periodicals, Modern Language Association International Bibliography, Guide to Social Science and Religion in Periodical Literature, and Pastoral Care and Counseling Abstracts.

LC 77-647452   ISSN 0070-9801   JPJUD 6(1)1-76(1981)

Editor's Perspective

This issue of the *Journal of Psychology and Judaism* focuses on a lingering problem affecting a significant segment of the Jewish population, the survivors of the Holocaust and their offspring.

Survivors themselves are, from a strictly behavioral perspective, a unique group. Because of what they endured, their entire life orientation has been affected. In the general population, hypochondriacal fears, depressive reactions, and fragile sense of self are usually not normal. But for the survivors, to live a life free from fears, anxieties, depression and uncertainty would not be normal. Having been shattered, traumatized, dehumanized, picking up all the pieces is for them an almost impossible task.

Yet this does not mean that all survivors are "cases," or that they have only left a legacy of psychological disturbance. Survivors have lent a sense of balance and perspective; through their harrowing experiences they remain teachers of the difference between real and imaginary crisis or misery.

Through such outstanding human beings as Viktor Frankl, survivors have shared with the world a sense of hope and an unshakeable commitment to the unconditional meaningfulness and value of life, in any and all circumstances. It is important to keep in mind the positive contributions of survivors to the general equilibrium of society when approaching a study of post-Holocaust psychological problems.

The articles which comprise this issue combine the past, present, and future. Analysis of literature published in the past is used to understand the situation in the present and focus on methods of approach which may enhance the future of survivors and their offspring.

Elana Kuperstein, in the opening article, surveys the literature on adolescents of parent survivors. The presentation is in two parts, the first dealing with the clinical, the second with the meta-clinical realm. Her analysis forms a useful foundation for the articles which follow.

Leo Eitinger, a member of the editorial board, follows with a comparison of Norwegian survivors and survivor refugees who were admitted to Norway. Via this comparison Eitinger argues forcefully for a better understanding of the plight of the survivors.

Jack Nusan Porter takes up the baton from Eitinger in his investigation of whether there exists a psychological survivor's syndrome, not only among victims of the Holocaust, but also among their children. His research into the existence of a socio-political syndrome indicates that some positive human expressions are coming forth from children of survivors.

Florabel Kinsler, sensitive to the issues raised here and in many other books and articles, addresses herself to the specific needs of clients who are offspring of survivors. The basic thrust of her piece focuses on the short-term group treatment program she has been instrumental in developing so that the negative features of the post-Holocaust reality can be countered.

Stanley Schneider concludes this issue with a concise overview of a treatment program for adolescents of survivor parents. His therapeutic model is closely linked with a geographic factor, namely that the treatment takes place in Israel. This is considered vital for allowing positive identity goals.

These contributions are new additions to the already vast and continually expanding literature on the aftermath and aftereffects of the Holocaust. It is hoped that these pieces, individually and as a collective unit, will add to the understanding of this situation and help to channel post-Holocaust energies in a meaningful direction.

Reuven P. Bulka
Editor

Adolescents of Parent Survivors of Concentration Camps: A Review of the Literature

ELANA EIZAK KUPERSTEIN received an M.S. in Secondary Education from Indiana University, and a B.A. in English Literature from Queens College, New York. She is presently employed as a teacher of Hebrew and Jewish Studies in Pittsburgh, Pa. Born in Israel, her interest in adolescents of parent survivors of concentration camps is partially due to the fact that both her parents are survivors of the Holocaust.

ABSTRACT: This presentation is a survey of the literature concerning adolescents of parent survivors of concentration camps, and is divided into two parts. The first is mostly clinical literature based on observations of adolescents of survivors who have sought psychiatric help. The image of the adolescent child of survivors which emerges from these studies is that of one with severe problems. Two aspects of adolescence seem to be seriously affected; the process of achieving independence from parents, and the process of forming a separate and positive self-image. The second group of studies on this topic reveal an image of the adolescents of survivors which is much healthier psychologically. These are descriptive and journalistic accounts of lives of families of survivors written mostly by children of survivors.

Many studies have been published concerning survivors of Nazi concentration camps, but recently there has been a growing interest in the children of these survivors and their problems. Were the children of the victims also affected by the painful experiences of their parents? All studies agree that there has been an impact on these children, but they differ in their evaluation of the extent and the behavioral manifestations of this impact. Since this influence is transferred to the child through relationship with parents, it seems to be most pronounced at the time of adolescence, when the parent-child relationship changes and many of the adolescent's feelings, problems and values are being tested by him/her. This claim is further supported by the fact that most studies on this problem started appearing in the late sixties and early seventies, just as the children of most survivors were reaching adolescence. Those first studies were indeed a direct reaction to adolescent children of survivors who experienced certain problems and sought psychiatric help.

Were the adolescent tasks faced by children of survivors of concentration camps more difficult for them to master than for the average adolescent? Were their adolescent problems and concerns different or special in any way? Did they share common adolescent experiences unique to their group? This paper will present a review of the literature which attempts to answer these questions and to describe the nature of the common concerns of adolescent children of survivors.

Adolescence will be defined as a transitional period in development during which young people attempt to achieve physical, intellectual, social and emotional independence. As they try to form their own identity, they move from childlike behavior to mature behavior. This period is usually characterized by some degree of conflict which results from the rapid physiological and emotional changes which the adolescent must deal with. Adolescence cannot be set within limits of age, but it usually takes place from the beginning of "puberty" to "maturity" (Lambert, 1972, p. 6).

II

The literature on this topic can be divided into two distinct groups. The first, which also appeared first chronologically, consists mostly of clinical studies of psychiatric patients. Some of them are attempts at controlled studies, but even then most of the subjects are clinical patients. Some of these studies reached results which assigned serious pathological problems to the second generation of survivors.

These results, however, must be considered with some reservations. Many of the studies used sample groups which were too small. Most of them used clinical patients for the subjects and for the control groups so that their samples were not representative, and therefore the results cannot be attributed to the general population of survivors. The most common problem encountered while dealing with this topic is that the factors which contribute to the behavior observed cannot be easily determined, and certainly can be more or different than the single factor of having a parent survivor. This problem was not adequately treated or even mentioned by some of these studies.

The variables influencing the child of a survivor may be attributed to a number of factors. One contributing factor is that most of the parent survivors also belong to a Jewish immigrant group. The effect of growing up in different environments must also be dealt with. Another important variable is the personality of the parent and of the child, and to what extent it has contributed to the observed behavior.

Any attempt at forming scientific theories and generalizations concerning a painful and horrible human experience presents sensitive problems. How can one measure how much pain and suffering was inflicted and how much of its impact was left imprinted on human lives, and still remain scientifically objective in attitude? Should one even attempt to be objective about the horrors of concentration camps and try to assess how weak or strong the victims were before their camp experience? Vivian Rakoff responds to this problem:

> However strong or weak they were before they went into the nightmare, it seems inconceivable to me that men should not have been broken in some way by the accumulation of horrors which were more than men were made to endure. If someone walked on eggs and they broke nobody would complain that they were fragile. Eggs are not made to be walked on. (Rakoff, 1966, p. 18)

Thus, when considering the results of these studies, their limitations must be remembered.

The second group of published literature on this topic appears a bit later than the first, and aims at slightly different goals. While most studies in the first group aim at reaching statistically and scientifically validated conclusions on the effect of a parent survivor on a child, the second group has more modest goals. It only tries to voice and describe the conflicts and feelings shared by some children of survivors, who believe that it is important for them to discuss these problems and to write about them. Most of them are not clinical patients, but have been aware of a certain aspect of their lives that makes them different, or that separates them from others. This group presents personalized and vivid accounts and interviews by and about a number of children of survivors.

Vivian Rakoff (1966) states that although many of the survivors of concentration camps seem to lead normal lives, the long term effects of the concentration camp experience lead to severe psychiatric symptomatology in the adolescent children of these survivors. He describes three case histories of his adolescent patients, each of whom is an only child of survivor parents, who in turn are the only survivors of their families. Until adolescence these children were relatively good and obedient, but with the onset of adolescence they became phobic, wild and hysterical, or depressed. Two of them even tried to put an end to their lives.

Rakoff feels that these children see their parents as sacred figures because of their suffering, and therefore suffer guilt when they rebel or disobey. They cannot express the normal aggression towards their parents as they grow up, so that when adolescence demands the expression of independence, their anger finally emerges in distorted and violent forms. These adolescents also complain of being overly protected by their parents, they complain of depression and gloom at home, and most of all they complain of excessive expectations. The survivor parents who see life as an unexpected gift, see the lives of their children as missions in which the child has to compensate for the lives of all the dead ones, justify the survival of the parents, and gratify the hopes and expectations which are usually gratified by mothers, fathers, sisters, brothers, cousins, etc.

Trossman (1968) feels that the adolescent child of survivors is affected if one or both of the parents suffer from even a mild form of the Survivor Syndrome. The term "Survivor Syndrome" attempts to group together certain common problems shared by concentration camp survivors, most of whom exhibit one or more of the behaviors it describes. Since many of these problems directly affect the child of the survivor, they are of great significance to this study.

According to Krystal and Niederland (Krystal, 1968, pp. 327-340), the predominant aspects of this syndrome include anxiety and phobia of all kinds, severe cases of nightmares and continued disturbances or hallucinations upon waking, chronic depression often associated with or caused by survivor guilt, feelings of isolation and inability to enjoy life, and pain caused by psychosomatic disease.

Trossman (1968) states that an adolescent child of a parent who suffers from this "syndrome" is likely to exhibit some of the following behavior. Because the parents are over-protective and constantly warn their child of impending danger, the adolescent either becomes phobic or tries to rebel against their phobia. Sometimes the child is used as an audience for the continuous recounting of painful memories of the parents and as a result becomes depressed or feels guilty for having a better fortune. In one case the parents called their child by derogatory names that were used to refer to them in the camps, and in so doing damaged the child's self-esteem.

Some Jewish parents feel hostile and mistrustful towards the gentile world and their children either adopt this feeling, or rebel against it by insisting on dating non-Jews. These parents invest enormous expectations in their child, who is the symbol of the new world for them, and the child often develops anxiety or rebels against this pressure. Examination anxiety is a behavior that results from pressure of parents on the child to do well in college. Education is important, and the child is sent to college even when the parents can hardly afford it. When taking a test, the student often panics since he/she is aware of the great emotional investment in this examination.

Another problem encountered by the late adolescent is related to sex role identification. A parent who suffers from depression and a feeling of isolation becomes preoccupied and leaves all family responsibilities for the other parent. This creates problems similar to those of a family with an absent parent. If the emotionally-absent parent is of the same sex as the adolescent, problems are created in the formation of the sexual identity of the adolescent. Trossman based his observations on students who came for help at the McGill Student Mental Health Clinic. He suggests the necessity for further study of this problem, especially for comparison with non-patient subjects and for comparison with children of survivors who were not in concentration camps.

In his study of adolescents of survivors of concentration camps, Rustin (1971) reported that they display more guilt than other children, and that they are more involved in Jewish identification than are other Jewish adolescents, since they identify very strongly with their parents.

Sigal and Rakoff (1971) compared thirty-two families where at least one parent was a concentration camp survivor to a control group of twenty-four families of European immigrant parents who were not concentration camp survivors. All families were Jewish. They found that the concentration camp families experienced more difficulty in controlling their children, they overvalued their children, and complained more about fights between siblings. The parents were preoccupied with the mourning for lost lives and emotionally too depleted to provide the proper limits demanded by the children. Feeling too guilty to show aggression to the already suffering parent, some children directed their anger towards their brothers and sisters.

Sigal (1971) reports of these same observations and compares them with similar patterns of parent-child interaction in families where the parents were traumatized in a different way, but shared the same psychological characteristics of survivors of concentration camps, especially in their pattern of preoccupation. Both studies stress that it is not the concentration camp experience itself that led to these manifestations, but rather the feeling of loss of important figures in the past and its effect on the parent's affective resources.

These authors include an important warning against considering these symptoms as an inevitable consequence of having a survivor parent in the family. They remind us that they have no data on the frequency of these patterns in the general survivor population, since their studies were based on patient subjects only. However, a more somber hypothesis is also presented by Sigal and Rakoff (1971):

> These findings, taken together with studies that abound in the literature indicating a relationship between disturbances in the parent-child relationship and later personality difficulties in the children, suggest that there is a distinct possibility that the children of the concentration camp group may themselves rear disturbed children so that the wartime experience of the concentration camp parents may adversely affect the functioning of children generations removed. (p. 396)

III

Sigal, Silver, Rakoff, and Ellin (1973) continued and extended this study on adolescents of survivors. These adolescents were found to display more behavioral and coping difficulties than the control group. They also suffered from a greater sense of alienation and from excessive dependency. Parental preoccupation is again seen as the predominant contributing factor.

Kestenberg (1972) emphasized the importance of other variables influencing the survivor parent which may affect the capability of raising children. Age during the war, the length of time of persecution, and pre-war experiences, may all affect capabilities as a parent. Again, she states that the concentration camp experience alone does not define a survivor parent. Having survived the Nazi persecution through hiding or any other means can also affect the parent psychologically. Incomplete mourning for lost relatives, objects, and a past identity can preoccupy the parent and interfere with a proper parent-child relationship.

This finding supports results of previous studies about the emotionally-absent parent. Since survivors used to behave as inconspicuously as they could on selection lines (Jaffe, 1970, p. 309), and tried to disappear in the mass and efface themselves (Bettelheim, 1960, pp. 210-211) in order to save themselves from being noticed and selected for death, some of them continue this practice and become the preoccupied or the emotionally-absent parent.

Developing a positive self-image is one of the crucial tasks of adolescence. Kestenberg emphasizes that parents who suffered from an irrational, racial rejection and persecution by their environment, especially as adolescents, may have developed a feeling of self-hatred and worthlessness that if left unchanged could later affect the proper development of a positive self-image in their adolescent children. Jaffe (1970, p. 313) also wrote about the basic feeling of self-depreciation and self-hatred in survivors which resulted from continuous degradation and de-individualization practiced in Nazi concentration camps. Inmates were forced to lose all dignity and self-esteem and often retained the hate towards this non-human image of themselves.

Adolescents were especially damaged by this kind of persecution, and among the most disturbed of camp survivors one finds those who were persecuted during adolescence (Krystal, 1968, p. 256). It is quite likely that such a parent will not be able to provide a positive and strong model of identification for the adolescent child.

Krystal and Niederland (1971) describe families of survivors as "affect-lame." The survivors are filled with repressed aggression which produces outbursts of aggression in the second generation, especially in adolescence (Krystal, 1968, p. 334). The parents are impaired in their ability for nurturing children, and this often produces depression in the next generation. These problems of the survivor promote a symbiotic relationship with the child which interferes with the process of individuation (Krystal, 1968, p. 346). Since individuation and achieving independence are major tasks of adolescence, children of this age are especially affected by the problems of the survivor parent.

Rustin and Lipsig (1972) discuss methods of psychotherapy for adolescents of survivors designed to help them overcome this "symbiotic relationship" with their parents and the resulting difficulty in the process of individuation. They have found that these adolescents often suffer from aspects of their parents' survivor syndrome. They feel both guilt and anger toward their parents, and some, as in a case study which they describe, feel withdrawn, depressed, and have difficulty with their interpersonal relationships. The task of the therapist is to alleviate the patient's guilt concerning the parent's depression and pain, to be both supportive and firm, and to help the patient establish a sense of separate identity so that every failure of the child will not be seen as a catastrophic event in the life of the parent.

Barocas and Barocas (1973) emphasize that parent survivors often force the child into a destructive identification. They see the child as an extension of themselves or of a lost member of their family, and attempt to gratify their own needs through the child. This inhibits the growth of this child and interferes with its individuation. Even minor failures of the child may be seen as failures in the function of validating the existence and survival of the parent, and lead to depressive or adverse reactions in the child.

Klein (1971) studied families of survivors in an Israeli kibbutz. He stressed that parents have a fear of damage or danger to the child, and a fear of separation from the child. Children of survivors find it difficult to express anger towards their parents. However, there is a release for aggression in the frequent wars. Victory in wars has helped many survivors overcome their feelings of degradation, and fighting for a cause added meaning to their lives. The suffering of the parents is often seen as justified in that it brought about the rebirth of Israel. The children tend to admire and emphasize the heroic deeds in their parents' past, and are reluctant to discuss the suffering.

Stephen Karr (1973) studied 71 adolescents of survivors between 17 and 29 years of age. They were divided into three groups: adolescents of parents who were both in a concentration camp, adolescents of one parent-survivor, and adolescents whose parents escaped the Nazi persecution. The results were obtained through recorded group interviews and through psychological testing. The adolescents of both-parent survivors showed more acceptance of the values of their parents, especially in the area of religious identification. They felt some hostility toward their parents, complained that they overprotected them, but felt guilty about having these feelings. They sought more psychotherapy and were less educated than the members of the other two groups. Children of the first group also exhibited less impulse control and had a greater tendency to be depressed or anxious. Adolescents of both parents who escaped reacted less passively to the subject of the Holocaust, and were often actively involved with it. The author feels the need for comparison of effects in other persecuted groups and believes that treatment is needed not only to relieve problems in the second generation, but also to prevent future difficulties in the third generation.

IV

In *The Child in His Family* (Anthony & Koupernik, 1973, pp. 359-415) one finds the proceedings of a symposium on the subject of the children of the Holocaust. The symposium was held in Jerusalem in August of 1970 and included presentations by M. Laufer, L. Rosenberger, E. Furman, D.R. Aleksandrowicz, H. Klein, and J.J. Sigal.

Moses Laufer presented a case study of a boy whose father died in a concentration camp and whose mother died later during his adolescence. The boy suffered from depression, fantasies about his real father and the circumstances of his death, and an inability to mourn. As a young adult the boy was finally able to cope with living and stopped treatment. Conflicting comments were presented concerning Dr. Laufer's analysis of this case. Some participants in the symposium felt that the treatment was not yet complete, and that there were many more painful events in the family than just the concentration camp experience of the parents. One commentator felt that the boy's ability to cope as well as he did was influenced by the examples of endurance provided by the mother, the concentration camp survivor.

L. Rosenberger believes that children of survivors do not manifest a distinct psychopathology. There are differences in their behavior and problems which can be attributed to different handling by parents, and to different personality traits of parents and children. She presented the case study of a nineteen-year-old suffering from depression and problems in school. His behavior patterns in adolescence seemed to imitate the activities of his adolescent father during his concentration camp experience. In Dr. Laufer's study, as in this case, the adolescents had school problems and suffered from depression.

Dr. E. Furman too, stresses that so much is different in the case of each survivor family, and in the personalities and interactions involved, that generalizations about second generation effects may be meaningless unless seen in the context of individual cases. She describes the case of Danny, especially in the light of mothering and its effects on the child. Danny's mother went through the concentration camp experience in her late adolescence and that influenced her decisions about the manner of mothering her own baby. Much of Dr. Furman's success was attributed by her to her ability to speak the same language (literally and figuratively) as Danny's mother, and to provide guidance for initiating maternal development based on more realistic concepts. Dr. Furman believes in studying individual cases carefully and in avoiding generalizations on the subject of children of survivors.

Dr. Dov Aleksandrowicz believes that a statistical analysis of the impact of concentration camp traumatization on the second generation is unreliable because so many variables are involved in the relationship and circumstances within each family. He did find, however, that the problems of the child often relate to the emotional scars seen in the survivor-parent. He also reported some cases of one passive and one dominant parent (parental disequilibrium), with the possibility of resulting problems in sex role identification during adolescence. Many of the parents in this group experienced the concentration camps as adolescents and early separation from their parents made it difficult for some of them to identify with the parental role.

Dr. Klein studied families of survivors in a kibbutz in Israel where the rebirth of the State helped rebuild a new and stronger self-image for the survivor. He found that the children of these survivors replace lost relatives in the mind of their parents, are often overprotected, and high expectations are invested in them. Adolescence seems to be particularly difficult since the quest for emotional and sexual independence is not always understood by the parents, whose own adolescence was so different.

Dr. Sigal mentions some of the difficulties in the methodology of these studies, especially those encountered by the participants in this symposium in discovering consistent patterns in the families that they had studied. He emphasizes a certain consensus reached by some of the participants about the importance of a treatment which provides a warm supportive environment not only for the child, but also for the survivor-parent.

In conclusion, this symposium presented some detailed case studies of adolescents of survivors, reached some conclusions as to the importance of therapy which includes the parent, yet failed to distinguish common patterns unique to the families of concentration camp survivors. In fact, many of the participants were reluctant to establish such generalizations and emphasized that statistical analysis is impractical and unreliable because of the many variables involved that may be difficult to measure, difficult to isolate, or unrelated to the concentration camp experience.

Paul Matussek (1975) presented an extensive work on the consequences of internment in concentration camps. His random sample is made up of survivors who are both patients and nonpatients. Multiple variables were subjected to careful analysis and the results indicated that just as the concentration camp experience does not constitute a uniform stress variable, so reaction to this stress differs. Prior life of inmates, their individual dispositions and social factors are all linked to their ability to overcome concentration camp life.

One important finding of this study is particularly relevant to the effect the survivor parent has on the child. The mother-child relationship of the survivor was found to have a great influence on the ability to confront later stress, such as concentration camp survival, and on post-persecution family life (Matussek, 1975, p. 249). This supports the hypothesis (Sigal & Rakoff, 1971, p. 396) that disturbed survivors may pass on their problems to future generations through their impaired relationship with their children.

The image of the adolescent of a survivor which emerges from most of these studies is that of one with severe problems. Two aspects of adolescence seem to be seriously affected; the process of achieving independence from parents, and the process of forming a separate and a positive self-image. The adolescent of a parent who suffers from the "survivor syndrome" may develop problems whether rebelling or identifying with the parents.

The tendency of this parent to overvalue the child and burden it with impossible expectations in the wish to live vicariously through the child, prevents the child from achieving its own goals, makes it feel inadequate, and places pressure against which the child often rebels at adolescence. The parent tends to have a phobia concerning the child, and over-protects him. This too leads to rebellion at adolescence when new experiences outside the home of the parents are sought after. The depressed and preoccupied parent, filled with a sense of loss and mourning, cannot deal properly with the burden of setting limits for the child, which causes behavior problems, and especially outbursts of aggression at adolescence.

Because the parent is seen as a depressed, suffering, and sometimes sacred figure, aggression and anger against the parent lead to excessive guilt and are sometimes held back indefinitely, or released suddenly at adolescence. If the anger against the parents is continuously held back, it interferes with the process of achieving gradual independence. If it is released suddenly, it is expressed in extreme, violent, and often dangerous ways.

The emotionally-absent or preoccupied parent may also present problems in sex role identification for the adolescent. The adolescent who does not rebel may identify with the parent to the extent of becoming depressed and tormented by anxiety and suspicions towards a hostile outside environment. According to most of these studies, it seems that the concentration camp effects are actually transferred to the second generation through the parent-child relationship.

V

In the second group of studies on this topic one discovers an image of the adolescents of survivors that is much healthier psychologically. These are descriptive journalistic accounts of lives of families of survivors written by the children of the survivors. Mostly, they describe the general population of children of survivors, those who have not sought psychiatric help, and as a result present adolescents who suffer from some of the problems described in the first group of studies, but in a milder form and accompanied by more modest and less destructive behavioral manifestations.

Lucy Steinitz and David Szonyi (1975) edited a collection of autobiographical, literary, and scholarly works on the subject, written by children of survivors. The personal accounts and conversations between these children of survivors—mostly young adults—present their view of the experiences and feelings which result from living with a survivor parent.

Dorothy Rabinowitz (1976) wrote about the new lives of a number of families of survivors who now live in the United States. Excerpts of interviews with them create a very intimate feeling of knowing these people. Most of them are very aware of the effect of the Holocaust on their lives, and some are still suffering from it.

Helen Epstein (1977) published an article in The New York Times Magazine entitled "The Heirs of the Holocaust." She outlined all the sensitive issues expressed by the people interviewed by her, and included her own feelings and experiences as a child of a survivor. She stressed the feeling of isolation, of being unique, or different, felt by many children of survivors in the United States, and the great relief they felt when voicing these intimate feelings and sharing them with others like them.

Epstein has recently completed a book on this subject, *Children of the Holocaust* (1979), in which she elaborates on the issues presented in her article, exposing more intimate and secret parts of her own experience as a child of survivors. She emphasizes the importance of sharing feelings with others of similar background, and confesses that opening up her "iron box" about the Holocaust released incredible feelings that she had always feared as a child. She interviewed American, Canadian, and Israeli young adults who are children of survivors, and described her own experience as a student in Israel. Although she approaches the psychological definitions of the second generation "effects" with caution, she recognizes that most of the people she interviewed make certain choices and carry a particular "world view" which is influenced by their parents' wartime experiences.

Bella Savran and Eva Fogelman (1979) describe the therapeutic awareness groups which they have formed for children of survivors. In these groups members could share their thoughts, and in so doing alleviate their sense of isolation. Through improved awareness many became better equipped to deal with some of the problems they discussed. The concerns expressed by members of these groups included feelings of being different or scarred, conflicts about their Jewish identify, combined feelings of guilt and anger towards their parents, and difficulty in separation from parents.

The issues discussed by most of the writers of the second group of studies on the subject included the quest for independence and the subsequent guilt, the relationship and attachment to the parents and their values, feelings toward Germans, experiences of persecution and phobia, feelings of isolation, identification with Judaism or with Israel, depression or sadness, and influences of the parents' experiences on choices of career and education.

A major goal of adolescence, independence, is more difficult for children of survivors whose parents suffered so many losses, and trying to claim that independence often results in guilt. Anita Norich writes, "When we think of moving away, we think of the losses our parents have had. How many losses can you impose on them?" (Steinitz & Szonyi, 1975, p. 49).

Guilt is sometimes aroused through the phenomenon of the "impossible comparison." The children compare themselves to the way their parents were as adolescents and feel that their concerns, goals and problems are very insignificant in comparison to the "life and death" type of concerns their parents experienced at that age. They feel that they have not suffered enough, and that their lives are too simple, easy, and free of worry. They feel inferior in their strength or capacity to endure hardship. Lucy Steinitz (Steinitz & Szonyi, 1975, p. 46) spoke about this comparison; "Also, I feel that I can never complain about my own troubles, because when compared to what my parents went through they're nothing." Toby Mostysser wrote, "And I knew for myself that any horrors of my own, any loneliness, or want, or frustration, paled before what my parents had suffered" (Steinitz & Szonyi, 1975, p. 6).

Children of survivors may view their parents as victims, heroes, or martyrs, but they are usually aware of a feeling of sadness which recurs in the parent. In *New Lives* (Rabinowitz, 1976) Elizabeth K., a survivor, speaks of this sadness; "There is always this sadness inside you, underneath everything"(p. 205).

Many adolescents experience conflicts regarding their Jewish identity. The fact that their parents were victimized purely on the basis of their race has many different effects on the parent and the child. Whether the adolescents reject Judaism or not, in most cases they have a very strong sense of being Jewish, because of their parents' experiences, and almost regardless of their religious convictions. These adolescents may rebel against religion, yet they usually come back to see themselves as Jews, and those who are not devoted in the religious sense still retain cultural ties to their heritage. Some become supporters of Zionism and of Israel. It is almost as if Hitler's persecution has singled their families out as Jews, and made them forever aware of their being Jewish.

Israel's struggles and wars awaken a feeling of Jewish identification in some of these adolescents and provide a certain sense of pride. Toby Mostysser (Steinitz & Szonyi, 1975, p. 17) writes about her rejection of the values of her parents, her need to escape their world, to travel and study foreign subjects, and about her return to it which was instigated by the 1973 war in Israel. "I responded to the war exactly as my parents did. And identification after years of my going my own way, sent me spinning." She was shocked by the passion of her response to the war, which she immediately associated with the "previous war against the Jews" in Europe. Even though she has no religious conviction, in the cultural sense she feels herself a Jew, and is very sensitive to all issues involving Jews (Steinitz & Szonyi, 1975, p. 19).

In conclusion, the second group of studies presents interviews with adolescents of parent-survivors who share common concerns and interests. It is important to remember that although commonly shared characteristics were definitely assessed, every story was unique. Every parent was affected by war experiences in a different way, a result of unique personality, disposition, values and socioeconomic background.

The same variables also affect the children. The foremost task that these adolescents must contend with is successfully separating their own lives, ideas, and interests from those of their parents. The obstacles they encounter include high parental expectations, overvaluing and overprotecting the child, and excessive guilt on the part of the child. They need to somehow reconcile their independence and wishes for fullfillment with the strong ties they will always feel to the parents. In so doing they must find the middle road between violent and extreme forms of rebellion and strong identification, which may also be destructive. They have to learn about the experiences of their parents, understand their significance, accept and remember them, yet they cannot allow themselves to be tormented by them, or to adopt whatever anxieties or phobia their parents may be suffering from as a result of the war. As Liliane Richman put it (Steinitz & Szonyi, 1975, p. 135), "I have both successfully remembered and forgotten the legacy my mother bequeathed me."

References

Anthony, E. & Koupernik, C. (Eds.). *The child in his family: The impact of disease and death* (Vol. 2). New York: John Wiley and Sons, 1973.

Barocas, H. & Barocas, C. Manifestations of concentration camp effects on the second generation. *American Journal of Psychiatry*, 1973, *130*(7), 820-821.

Bettelheim, B. *The informed heart: Autonomy in a mass age.* Glencoe, Illinois: The Free Press, 1960.

Epstein, H. *Children of the holocaust: Conversations with sons and daughters of survivors.* New York: G. P. Putnam's Sons, 1979.

Epstein, H. The heirs of the holocaust. *The New York Times Magazine,* June 19, 1977, pp. 12-15; 76-77.

Jaffe, H. The sense of guilt within holocaust survivors. *Jewish Social Studies,* 1970, *32*(4), 307-314.

Karr, S. *Second generation effects of the Nazi holocaust.*Unpublished doctoral dissertation, California School of Professional Psychology, San Francisco, 1973.

Kestenberg, J. Psychoanalytic contributions to the problem of children of survivors from Nazi persecution. *Israel Annals of Psychiatry and Related Disciplines,* 1972, *10*(4), 311-315.

Klein, H. Families of survivors in the kibbutz: Psychological studies. In H. Krystal & W. Niederland (Eds.), *Psychic traumatization.* Boston: Little, Brown, 1971.

Krystal, H. (Ed.). *Massive psychic trauma.* New York: International Universities Press, 1968

Krystal, H. & Niederland, W. (Eds.). *Psychic traumatization.* Boston: Little, Brown, 1971.

Lambert, G., Altman, R.; Green, L.B.; & Rothschild, B. *Adolescence: Transition from childhood to maturity.* Monterey, California: Brooks, Cole Publishing Co., 1972.

Matussek, P., Grigat R.; Haibock, H.; Halbach, G.; Kommler, R.; Mantell D.; Triebel, A.; Vardy, M.; & Wedel, G. *[Internment in concentration camps and its consequences.] D. & I. Jordan (trans.). New York & Berlin: Springer Verlag, 1975.*

Rabinowitz, D. *New lives: Survivors of the holocaust living in America.* New York: Alfred A. Knopf, 1976.

Rakoff, V. Long term effects of the concentration camp experience. *Viewpoints,* 1966,*1* 17-21.

Rustin, S. *Guilt, hostility and Jewish identification amongst adolescent children of concentration camp survivors.* Unpublished doctoral dissertation, New York University, 1971.

Rustin, S. & Lipsig, F. Psychotherapy with the adolescent children of concentration camp survivors. *Journal of Contemporary Psychotherapy,* 1972, *4*(2), 87-94.

Savran, B. & Fogelman, E. Therapeutic groups for children of holocaust survivors. *International Journal of Group Psychotherapy,* 1979, 29(2), 211-235.

Sigal, J. Second-generation effects of massive psychic trauma. In H. Krystal & W. Niederland (Eds.), *Psychic traumatization.* Boston: Little, Brown, 1971.

Sigal, J. & Rakoff, V. Concentration camp survival: A pilot study of effects of the second generation. *Canadian Psychiatric Association Journal,* 1971, *16*(5), 393-397.

Sigal, J.; Silver, D.; Rakoff, V.; & Ellin, B. Some second-generation effects of survival of the Nazi persecution. *American Journal of Orthopsychiatry,* 1973, *43*(3), 320-327.

Steinitz, L. & Szonyi, D. (Eds.). *Living after the holocaust: Reflections by the post-war generation in America.* New York: Bloch Publishing Co., 1975.

Trossman, B. Adolescent children of concentration camp survivors. *Canadian Psychiatric Association Journal,* 1968, *13*(2), 121-123.

Studies on Concentration Camp Survivors: The Norwegian and Global Contexts

LEO EITINGER received his medical degree from Masaryk University in 1937 and Ph.D. from the University of Oslo in 1958. Presently professor and superintendent at the University Psychiatric Clinic in Oslo, he was president of the Norwegian Psychiatric Association from 1964 to 1967, and is the author of numerous books and countless articles on various aspects of psychology and psychiatry, including incisive studies of the effects of the holocaust on survivors. He is a member of the editorial board of the Journal of Psychology and Judaism.

ABSTRACT: A short description of the Norwegian concentration camp survivors and of the fate of the Scandinavian Jews during World War II is given. The Jewish survivors in Norway are a tiny group with many traits in common with other Jewish survivors, such as loss of families, death sentence and persistent fear of death. On the other side they have some quite specific traits which are quite unique, such as favorable economic conditions, return to warm emotional relations, and good social adjustment. A contrast to this group are the survivor refugees who were admitted to Norway on a charitable basis. They were burdened with the fate of refugees, the serious psychic traumata from war-time, and their somatic illnesses which handicapped them. Even concentrated medical, psychiatric and social efforts to help them resulted in only short-lived success, because the full impact of their experiences was not understood. The many social, medical and psychological problems involved make it imperative to convey the message of the Holocaust and its tragic consequences to both scientific workers and the general public.

The fate of the Jews of the Scandinavian countries during World War II was somewhat different from that of the other European countries. Sweden was not occupied by the Nazis, and the Jewish population there had organized already before the war, and especially at its end, an impressive organization for helping refugees who came to Sweden. In the beginning it was mainly refugees from Germany, Austria and Czechoslovakia. Then the Norwegian and Danish refugees came, and finally the country threw its doors wide open in order to admit all the survivors from the Nazi concentration camps who were able to reach the Swedish ports.

In Denmark the Nazi-occupation was of a slightly more benign character than in the other countries. For a relatively long time the legal Danish government was able to exercise its power, while the Germans concentrated mainly on the military duties. During this period, an underground movement was organized, and it was only in the second part of 1943 that the total political situation in Denmark was changed in that the Germans also took over the political power. The consequence of this fact was that the extermination of the Jews that had been carried out all over Europe, now also was to be accomplished in Denmark. However, the well organized underground was able to interfere with these plans. Nearly the total Jewish population was hidden by an until then unheard of activity of thousands and thousands of Danish, who managed to "snatch away" the victims from the Germans and bring them safely to Sweden. Even the relatively small group of Danish Jews who were captured, partly because they did not want to go in hiding, were sent to the ghetto of Terezin (Theresienstadt) where they enjoyed a privileged status, and even were visited by representatives of the Danish Red Cross. The mortality of this group was not higher than can be expected in an average population.

In Norway, on the other hand, the Jewish population constituted only a tiny minority, less than one half pro-mille of the total Norwegian population. Nevertheless the Nazis started a ferocious antisemitic propaganda campaign and persecution, which culminated in deportation in 1942. Also in Norway the underground movement started a rescue action, but succeeded to save only about half of the population. Of the approximately 1,500 Jewish victims to be, about 50% managed to escape to Sweden, often under very dramatic and extremely difficult conditions, while the other half were caught and deported to the extermination camps in Germany. The 760 deported consisted of 100 refugees who had come to Norway from Central Europe before the war; the rest were Norwegian-born Jews. Of the last mentioned group, only 11 (1.7%) survived and returned to Norway. This appallingly low number of survivors was a "quantitee negligible" when the medical and psychological results of the survivor population were investigated in Norway. In Norway there were very seldom random mass arrests, and deportation of hostages occurred relatively rarely. This means that most of the persons who were arrested in Norway represent, to a certain extent, a positive selection of the whole population. They were the individuals who during the war were risking their lives and physical freedom in order to contribute to keeping up morale and resistance in the people by—at that time—illegal activities. They secretly printed newspapers, tried to escape from the country in order to join the allied forces, helped people, among them Jews, to escape to Sweden, and collected information for the allies, etc. Physically and psychically they were a somewhat positive selection of the total population, persons who had been in full activity before they were arrested. After the liberation, they were brought to Norway, received with open arms by the population as war victims and given the necessary immediate medical help. After that, however, everybody, including themselves, expected that they should continue their prewar work as if nothing had happened. The majority really tried to reassume their work after a comparatively short holiday. It soon turned out that their working capacity was reduced, and a large scale investigation of Norwegian concentration camp survivors was initiated by a team of doctors connected with the Oslo University medical school.

Earlier Investigations

The author has been a member of this team during its entire period of work, and has in addition to that investigated more than 2,000 concentration camp survivors. They have been either inpatients or outpatients at the psychiatric department of the Oslo University hospital, or they have applied for disability pensions in Norway or Germany. The last applies especially to refugees who came to Norway after World War II. In addition to that, the author has been in Israel, where he has examined concentration camp survivors at psychiatric outpatient departments in all the mental hospitals there, and has worked as a consultant for the restitution organization. The detailed results of all these investigations have been published elsewhere in a number of larger monographs and papers (Eitinger, 1972). In addition to this, the author, together with professor Axel Stróm, has investigated the mortality and the morbidity of the total survivor population (Eitinger & Strom, 1973).

The Norwegian Survivors

For the sake of general overview, it can be stated here that the ex-prisoners had a markedly higher mortality rate in the postwar years than expected. The excess mortality rate was higher just after liberation, but has also been marked in all later periods until 1975, when our last investigation was concluded. Without going into details, it can be stated that the ex-prisoner population had a social development which was characterized by a decline, in contrast to the successful and positive economic trend characterizing the average Norwegian population. Their ability to succeed in occupational life also deteriorated in comparison with the prewar ability. In addition to this, it could be shown beyond any doubt that the ex-prisoners had been sick more often than the controls, that the greater morbidity among the ex-prisoners is not restricted to any special diagnosis, that the ex-prisoner's sick periods and hospitalization periods were about three times as long as those of the controls, and that the average number of sick leaves per person, sick days per person and sick days per sick leave were greater for the ex-prisoners than for the controls.

It could be demonstrated furthermore that the ex-prisoners' higher mortality and morbidity can be explained most naturally by the fact that the excessive stress they had experienced during imprisonment lowered their resistance to infections and lessened their ability to adjust to difficult environmental changes. Even small additional stress situations were able to upset their labile equilibrium, and resulted thus in a manifest illness. The more important finding was that this reduced ability to adjust and the weakened resistance did not change very much during the observation period. It seems that the traumatization during the stay in the camps was so profound that total recovery was not possible. This altered the ex-prisoners to a group of people who ever since the war have been more frequently and more seriously ill, and who consequently had a lower working capacity, lower incomes, and fewer possibilities for self-realization than a corresponding group of the population who had not experienced the same stress. The limited sentence that internment in a concentration or prison camp was intended to be has thus become a life-long sentence, affecting both the prisoners' life span and their health, if not their freedom.

As mentioned in the introduction, the Jewish survivors were of no quantitative importance in this Norwegian investigation. Nevertheless they represent a very interesting group because they have many factors in common with other Jewish survivors, especially those whom the author has interviewed in Israel. However, there is something quite unique in these few persons, which will be discussed in this presentation. The factors they have in common with the other Jewish survivors are: (1) the real fear of death which dominated all the

Jewish inmates because of the fact that their stay in the camp was to be considered a slow execution of the existing death sentences; and (2) they were exposed to the same extreme psychic shock experiences, being isolated completely from their families and being full of fear for their fate, very often suspecting, sometimes knowing that most of them have been killed.

The Jewish Survivors in Norway

Among the tiny group of Jewish survivors in Norway, every second one was the only surviving member of a total and often rather large family. The most extreme case was a man who had lost his parents and seven of his siblings in Auschwitz. This corresponds to the losses that have been found in the investigated survivors of concentration camps in Israel. Between 80 and 90% of them had lost the majority of their closest relatives, i.e. parents, siblings, husband or wife. Of the remaining 10-20%, more than two of the family had survived. There was not one single person among those investigated who had not lost at least one near relative. Between 75 and 80% were totally isolated at the end of the war, i.e. they were the sole survivors of their families. In addition to this, all the married persons had lost their children. The psychotraumatic importance contained in figures like these is difficult to understand fully.

In spite of the Norwegian Jewish survivors' being exposed to the same degree of family bereavement, their isolation was not the same as that seen in the displaced person camps in Europe. There more than half of the rescued and investigated population tried to get back to their home towns in the hope that in spite of everything, they still might find some members of the family. The hopelessness of this quest is best illustrated by the fact that the majority fled westward again during the course of 1945-46. This was partly owing to the hostile attitude of the local population, but mostly to the attempt to find someone of the family in the new DP-camps they had heard of. The Jewish survivors in Norway returned naturally to their homes, knowing that the Norwegian Jewish community was a very closely knit one, with family relations, kinship and friendship in all possible directions, encompassing the total population, nearly without exceptions. This meant that the returning survivors were accepted by those who had been able to escape to Sweden as near relatives, with all the warmth, acceptance and emotionality that was quite natural in those days. The question of survivor guilt was, naturally enough, never aired openly, but it is very reasonable to believe that the survivor guilt was stronger among those who had been rescued and had lived their lives relatively secure in Sweden, than among those who returned from the concentration camps.

Another important point of difference between the Norwegian Jewish survivors and those of Eastern Europe was their social and economic situation. The Norwegian government accepted compensation rules for the survivors immediately after the war, and their economic position was thus a relatively favorable one. None of them had any real economic problems. It must be supposed that they had been quite unusually resistant to have survived the camps, because detailed medical examinations have shown that they suffered from injuries and chronic diseases to about the same extent as the other Norwegian survivors. Unlike the other Norwegian survivors, however, their reduced capacity for work had little influence on their social adjustment, which seemed to be good. They were accepted, socially active members of their local communities, with families, friends and other social contacts. The explanation for their impressive achievement lies not only in their physical and mental power of resistance, but mainly in the support and protection generally offered them by their extended families and friends.

Survivor Refugees in Norway

Quite different, however, was the situation of the refugees who were admitted to Norway on a charitable basis. In contrast to many other countries, Norway did not primarily accept healthy, strong and ablebodied young people. On the contrary, people suffering from tuberculosis, blindness and other somatic diseases, and those whose working capacity was reduced, were favored by the immigration panels. Therefore, the burden born by the refugees in Norway has been manifold. They have serious psychic traumata from wartime, and somatic illnesses which handicap them in competition with other workers. On top of all this, they are often completely isolated, strangers and refugees in a foreign country. They lack every form of anchorage in the community where it was hoped they would settle down and become rehabilitated.

Even if this group is towering in its tragedy, it is a quantitatively small one, and, just as the other Jewish survivors in Norway, has had little impact on the general understanding of the Holocaust in the

Scandinavian countries. It was supposed by many that the situation
would be a quite different one in the United States, where large
numbers of refugees were the dominant part of the survivor
population, and thus were able to convey a more realistic picture of
what had happened. The incorrectness of this assumption is clearly
illustrated by the studies on the Buffalo Creek disaster. A comparison
between our refugee patients/survivors and the victims of the Buffalo
Creek disaster seemed imperative, though not so for most of the
investigators who worked with the survivors of Buffalo Creek
(Erikson, 1976; Lifton & Olson, 1976).

For completeness sake, a few words about this disaster are in order.
On February 26, 1972, an enormous slag dam gave way and unleashed
thousands of tons of water and black mud on the Buffalo Creek valley
in southern West Virginia, and disturbed everything in its pass, killing
125 people and leaving 4,000 homeless. It expended its forces in no
more than 15 minutes at any one point in the 18 mile long valley. A
group of 644 survivors of this disaster started a legal action against
the company that owned the dam. Disabling psychiatric symptoms
such as anxiety, depression, changes in character and life style and
maladjustment and developmental problems in children, were in
evidence more than 2 years after the disaster in over 90% of the
individuals interviewed. A sociological study concluded that the
survivors of the Buffalo Creek disaster suffered both individual and
collective trauma, the latter being reflected in the loss of communality.
Human relationships in this community had been derived from
traditional bonds of kinship and neighborliness. But, forced to give up
long standing ties with familiar places and people, the survivors
experienced demoralization, disorientation, and loss of connection.
Stripped of the support they had received from the community, they
became apathetic and seemed to have forgotten how to care for one
another. It was furthermore stated that the traumatization did not
stop with the cataclysmic events of the flood, which was only the first
phase. The survivors were returned not to their familiar ground, but to
new and strange surroundings. This is considered as further
threatening, and the survivors continued to face challenges for a long
time and during a raw and vulnerable state. Furthermore, it was
stressed that there was an element in this disaster that is not present
in truly natural catastrophic events, namely the human element, the
thought and the accusation that this horrible occurrence could have
been prevented. This aroused impulses of aggression and retaliation.
Feelings of rage, impotence, anxiety, guilt and depression were added
to the usual response to the disaster.

It was interesting that among all the papers written about this disaster, only one (Lifton & Olson, 1976) referred to the literature of the Holocaust. It thus seems that the importance of this event has not been grasped sufficiently in the American literature either. In this author's view, a comparison can not be avoided. One has to imagine a flood lasting not only a few minutes, but several years, killing not 125, but 6 million people, a destruction caused not by human negligence, but by deeply fanatic and hateful monomania and by the wreckless determination of a destructive and paranoic dictator and his blind and obstinate followers. Furthermore, the destruction encompassed not 14 mining hamlets, but hundreds and hundreds of townlets, cities and communities. In addition to this, our survivors are not the greatest part of the total population, but they are only remnants, a handful of hopelessly isolated people, with chronic psychiatric and somatic traumatization and diseases. Like the survivors of the Buffalo Creek disaster, our survivors could not return to their familiar ground, but had to adjust to new and strange surroundings. Our survivors' new surroundings were most strange—new countries, new languages, new laws and new lives were the problems with which they were confronted.

In addition to this, it is important to stress the above mentioned family-disasters and the quite exceptional bearing of them on family in an eastern Jewish community. In support of this statement, it might be adequate to quote a few excerpts from the anthropological study by Zborowski and Herzog (1962):

> Family ties continue close even when one is no longer part of the household. Several times each year, aunts, uncles, cousins—the entire family . . . will gather to celebrate some event, or one of the holidays.
> Human relations are expected to endure. There is seldom a final end to anything. Certainly a brother is always a brother, a sister always a sister. There may be quarrels and misunderstandings, but in time of crisis a family hangs together and cares for its own. If parents cannot give their children the support and help that is their due, other members of the family are expected to step in. Perhaps an uncle, an aunt, a grandparent, or even a more remote relative will take responsibility. It is always assumed that those who can will do, and those who have will give.
> Nothing so strongly demonstrates the sense of family cohesion as the assumptions about help one can count on as a matter of course from relatives. It is taken for granted that if a brother's child is sick and the brother cannot pay for the best of attention, if he has a daughter to be dowered, a son to be educated, a more prosperous brother or sister

should shoulder the expense. It is "only natural" that the brother or sister who emigrates to the United States "can't rest" until he brings more of the family over. It may be less that he cannot bear to live without them than that one just "naturally" behaves so. At times, however, extreme personal devotion enters in.

Kinship ties, even distant ones, entitle an individual to food, lodging and support when he comes to visit. In a strange town or city you seek out a relative to stay with, and there is usually one to be found. He may be your uncle, your seventh cousin, or the nephew of your brother's mother-in-law. If a man needs a job, a wealthy relative must give him one if it is at all possible. If not, he must help him to find one.

Again, it cannot be assumed that the assistance is always joyously extended. On the contrary.... But again, there is no choice. The obligation is real and unalterable.

These mutual obligations act almost as a form of insurance in an economic system as unstable as that of the shtetl.

For the shtetl, the community is an extended family. (pp. 303-304, 306)

It seems appropriate to quote fully this description of the central position held by family cohesion in the minds of the refugee survivors in Norway. It will then be easier to understand that the total disintegration of this cohesion in the community and in the family would necessarily result in radical changes in the individual's apprehension both of the self and the surroundings.

Only this background explains completely why an extremely comprehensive and concentrated medical, psychiatric and social effort was necessary in order to help people so severely traumatized back into a life of work. Nevertheless, the full impact of their experiences was not grasped by the authorities and complete help thus could not be given. Even if the rehabilitation in the first years could be considered a success, and even if they received continual systematic help, the results must be considered as very labile, and deteriorating from year to year.

This situation has been worsened in the last years by the more obvious aggressivity which is demonstrated by the anti-Israel political world and by the growing neo-Nazi movement. Even if, from a rational point of view, these political changes have no bearing on the individual refugee, it is obvious that these patients are extremely sensitive to the slightest variations of the political atmosphere and to the total attitude towards the existence of the State of Israel. Anxiety reactions in these patients have become quite general and disabling. Their nightmares are more frequent and often just as frightening as they had been immediately after the war. The seriousness of the

Holocaust traumatization is seen in that nearly all the refugees who came to Norway under the scheme of charitable transports and who have been rehabilitated in the first years after their arrival, are by now to be considered as disabled, without working capacity. In the long run, the efforts of all the social agencies and rehabilitation workers, together with the often serious efforts of the survivors themselves, have not been strong enough to overcome completely the evils of the past—and the present.

The experiences with our least privileged or most underprivileged group of survivors, seems to be a strong indicator and a serious challenge to convey the message of the Holocaust and its tragic consequences to both scientific workers and the general public.

References

Eitinger, L. *Concentration camp survivors in Norway and Israel.* The Hague: Martinus Nijhoff, 1972.

Eitinger, L. & Strom, A. *Mortality and morbidity after excessive stress: A follow-up investigation of Norwegian concentration camp inmates.* Atlantic Highlands, New Jersey: Humanities Press, 1973.

Erikson, E. Loss of communality at Buffalo Creek. *American Journal of Psychiatry,* 1976, *133*(3), 302-305.

Lifton, R. & Olson, E. The human meaning of total disaster: The Buffalo Creek experience. *Psychiatry,* 1976, *39*(1), 1-18.

Zborowski, M. & Herzog, E. *Life is with people.* New York: Schocken Books, 1962.

Is There a Survivor's Syndrome?
Psychological and Socio-Political Implications

JACK NUSAN PORTER, presently Boston director of AMPAL—American-Israel Securities Corporation, received his B.A. from the University of Wisconsin-Milwaukee in 1967 and his M.A. and Ph.D. in sociology from Northwestern University in 1971. He is the author, editor, or co-editor of fourteen books and nearly 150 articles, and among his most recent works are The Jew as Outsider, The Sociology of American Jews, Jewish Partisans: A Documentary of Jewish Resistance During WW II, Conflict and Conflict Resolution: A Sociological Introduction, and Jews in Cults: An Annotated Bibliography. He is the founder of the Journal of the History of Sociology and editor of the International Conflict and Cooperation Newsletter. The son of Holocaust survivors, Dr. Porter was born in Rovno, Ukraine during the war. He has written and lectured widely on comparative genocide, the impact of the Holocaust on survivors and their children, Jewish resistance, and the resurgence of neo-Nazism today.

ABSTRACT: An analysis of the children of survivors and their parents through the use of sociological observation and examination of the literature is presented, showing that there exists a psychological survivor's syndrome among the victims of the Holocaust. Also, the basis for a socio-political syndrome is indicated. As for the children of survivors, most of whom are now between 20-35 years of age, there is not enough data to say for sure, but it is highly unlikely that a pathological syndrome exists, though a mild secondary guilt syndrome may appear in some cases. More research with larger samples is necessary. As for a socio-political syndrome, superficial observation yields that a large number of children of survivors are committed to making sense out of the Holocaust and this can lead to a wide variety of creative political and religious actions. Also presented are some observations on the third generation of survivors, the offspring of the children of a section of the original survivors.

Funding for this research came from the Wein Foundation of Chicago under the direction of Dr. Byron Sherwin of Spertus College. This article is a greatly expanded version of a paper which appeared in the anthology, *Encountering the Holocaust,* edited by Byron Sherwin and Susan Ament (Impact Press/Hebrew Publishing Co., 1979). Reprint permission from Byron Sherwin (Ed.). An earlier version of this paper was read at the Second International Victimology Conference, held at Northeastern University in Boston, in September 1976. Thanks to Dr. Robert Ravven and the staff of the Countway Medical Library of Harvard University for their support and assistance.

The purpose of this paper is to present a survey of the highlights of the socio-psychological literature concerning the aftereffects of the Holocaust upon survivors and their children, and to answer the question whether there exists a "survivor's syndrome" among both survivors and their children. Furthermore, this paper will introduce a new concept, the socio-political syndrome among survivors and their offspring. In short, it will try to answer the question whether one can generalize about a socio-political syndrome as well as a psychological syndrome among these two groups.

Literature in this area divides into two parts, each overlapping the other; psycho-analytical case studies written by psychologists and psychiatrists and personal memoirs or journalistic accounts written by survivors themselves or by sympathetic writers. Though a significant body of literature exists, most of it is based on small clinical samples. There is a great deal of work to be done not only by psychologists but by sociologists and political scientists in order to expand our knowledge of survivors. Researchers in the past too often emphasized severe pathology not only of the first generation but the second generation of survivors as well. This paper questions whether a "pathological" approach is sufficient. It proposes that social psychological and sociological studies be developed in order to examine those survivors and their children who function normally and who are not beset by severe psychological problems. In other words, the socio-political aspects of these groups must also be examined in order to round out the picture of Holocaust survivors.

Disaster Studies: An Overview

Generally, studies of the Holocaust victims fall under the broad category of disaster research. These studies contain several labels— "trauma research," "stress or seige studies," "collective behavior," "catastrophe studies," and "disaster research." There are four major approaches which scientists take (Grossen, Welchsler, and Greenblatt, 1969).

General Systems Theory is concerned with the structure and process of systems of social phenomena. The concepts of adaptation to stress, equilibrium maintenance in reaction to such stress, information-processing, inputs, and outputs are all used in this approach. General systems theory is useful in precisely defining and manipulating social variables within a given system, especially through the use of computers and statistical models. It is an important tool in research and should be used more widely in this field but I find the approach too mechanical and consequently will not use it in this discussion.

Collective Behavior Theory is another popular approach to disaster studies. Collective behavior is actually a generic term for various social phenomena; crowds, riots, revolts, propaganda, public opinion, mass migration, and natural and man-made disasters. Such an approach emphasizes group morale, leadership, cohesiveness, collective defense, rumor control, and other manifestations of group behavior. This theoretical approach is also a useful tool but will not be stressed in this article.

Socio-Political Theory emphasizes the sociological, religious, cultural, political, and economic adaptations of survivors and victims to disaster. This approach will be widely used in the discussion of a possible "socio-political syndrome" among survivors and their children. This approach places the survivor in his/her normal socio-economic setting after the Holocaust and stresses the *positive* rather than the pathological adaptations of the victims.

Psycho-analytical Theory puts its major emphasis on individual reactions to stressful situations. The vocabulary of this approach concentrates on such concepts as trauma, emotional reaction, threat, defense, anxiety, guilt, and internal conflict. It is both a therapeutic and analytical approach; that is, it is both therapy and theory. Bruno Bettelheim, Viktor Frankl, Elie Cohen, Robert J. Lifton, William Niederland, Judith Kestenberg, H.Z. Winnik, Vivian Rakoff and John Sigal are the most widely-read figures in this field. This approach will be used in this paper in describing the "psychological syndrome" of survivors and their children.

One danger is to rely solely upon one approach. Each perspective gives only one view of the subject. It is necessary to utilize as many approaches as possible in order to obtain a complete picture. For example, the weakness of much of the Holocaust research is that it is rarely comparative. Concentration camp research is actually a subcategory of research on such total institutions as military prisons, POW camps, and civilian prisons. If Jews in such camps were compared to soldiers in POW camps, a more balanced and less defensive perspective could emerge. If the Jewish reaction to ghettoization and persecution were compared to reactions of civilians to such diverse phenomena as nuclear attack, natural disasters, air-raids, and collective panic, then research would show that the Jews reacted similarly to other groups (Grosser, Welchsler, and Greenblatt, 1964). If Jewish survivors could be compared to Armenian or Gypsy survivors, again a more balanced picture could be drawn. In short, the appearance of guilt and other psychological reactions are as normal for survivors of the Holocaust as they are for other survivors, of nuclear attack, natural disasters, war combat, or intense life-depriving accidents such as plane or car crashes.

What is a Survivor?

Before the outbreak of World War II, there were about 8.8 million Jews living in Europe. Approximately 5.8-6.2 million Jews were killed in the Holocaust. Of the three million who remained, it has been estimated that between 400,000-500,000 survived the war years in labor camps, in the partisans, hiding in caves, in the forests or the countryside. No more than 75,000 outlived the concentration camps (Epstein, 1977). Thus, there are about a half million or three million survivors depending on one's definition. I will adhere to the half-million figure: that is, *a survivor is someone who has survived an immediate and traumatic life-threatening experience.* Otherwise, one could say that all Jews everywhere were survivors because it was the Nazi aim to exterminate all of them. But this, while true in a metaphorical sense, would only confuse the issue.

We could say that there are about one-half million children of survivors in the world, the majority of them between 25-35 years old. Their parents range in age from 55 to 75, assuming they were between 20-40 years old when the war ended in 1945. The largest number of survivors went to live in Israel, with many coming to the United States and Canada, and with other large pockets of survivors in South America, England, France, and the Soviet Union. Many of these survivors and their children live in distinct communities set apart not only from the non-Jewish, but also from the already established Jewish community.

The label of survivor will be used for anyone who experienced life-threatening traumas and who left Europe in the 1930's—mostly German and Austrian Jews, as well as those who went through the DP camp experience and left in the late 1940's and early 1950's for Israel, Canada, the Americas, or other countries. The children of survivors are defined as those who are the offspring of survivors, whether or not these children experienced the Nazi trauma first-hand or not. That is, it includes those born in Europe during the war, those born in DP camps after the war, and those born in the "new" country long after the war.

This paper will outline the psychological symptoms of survivors and the socio-political coping behaviors of first-generation survivors. It will then explore the psychological and then the socio-political coping behavior of the children of survivors. Some feel that the Nazi trauma is re-experienced in the lives of the children and even the grandchildren of survivors. Is this true only for those who were death camp survivors or for all types of survivors? What is the magnitude, severity, and duration of these effects? How are these effects passed on to future generations? It may not be possible to answer all these questions in this paper, but they will be raised so that others can find an answer.

Clinical Symptomology of Holocaust Survivors

Psychiatrists have attempted to explain whether or not there exists an entity called the "survivor syndrome" and if so, what are its manifestations. One of the world's foremost authorities on psychic trauma, William G. Niederland, has outlined some of the primary and secondary characteristics of adults on whom repeated traumata has been inflicted (in Krystal & Niederland, 1971).

> Personality changes in the survivor of such experiences are related to quantitative factors. Massive traumatic experiences of this kind have devastating effects on the total ego organization. Most survivors suffer from chronic or recurrent depressive reactions often accompanied by states of anxiety, phobic fears, nightmares, somatic equivalents, and brooding ruminations about the past and lost-love objects.
> The sequelae of massive and repeated traumatization are:
> 1. Anxiety, usually associated with phobic or hypochondriacal fears, alone or in combination.
> 2. Disburbances of cognition and memory.
> 3. Chronic depressive reactions characterized by guilt, seclusion, and isolation.
> 4. Psychosomatic symptoms or disorders.
> 5. Psychosis-like or psychotic manifestations.
> 6. Life-long sense of heightened vulnerability to and increased awareness of dangerous situations.
> 7. Disturbances of sense identity, body-image, and self-image.
> 8. Permanent personality changes. (pp. 1-9)

Let us examine in more detail what Niederland calls the sequelae or aftereffects of traumatization.

Anxiety. This is the most common complaint and is associated with fear of renewed persecution. Victims manifest deep disturbances, phobias, anxiety dreams, and rerun nightmares. Chronic insomnia occurs due to these recurrent nightmares and anxieties.

Disturbances of cognition and memory. Amnesia, especially upon waking up from nightmares, is the most prevalent disturbance here.

Lost or bewildered states and a sense of disorientation from the present are also found.

Chronic depressive reactions. These reactions, from masochistic character changes to psychotic depression, cover a wide range. In their severity, the reactions are correlated to the intensity of survivor guilt based on the loss of loved ones.

Tendency to isolation, withdrawal, and brooding. Survivors are marked by unstable or difficult relationships and problems with intimacy. These psychological states manifest themselves in other social settings and victims often withdraw from political and community involvement.

Alterations of personal identity. These include impairment of body image and self-image and manifest themselves in frequent complaints of "I am a different person," "I am a weaker, more abhorrent person," or in some cases, "I am not a person." At its most extreme, the image of the *musselman* or living corpse appearance which some victims exhibit is an example of this alteration. Robert Lifton makes similar statements about Hiroshima survivors who exhibit a kind of psychic numbing, a closing-off of feelings, manifested by a macabre, shadowy, shuffling, and ghost-like impression. The all-encompassing psychological scar on the total personality is often a defense against death anxiety and death guilt. In milder forms it appears as sluggish despair consisting of diminished vitality, easy fatigability, "weakness," "exhaustion" of the nervous system, and "inadequate functioning of an organ or organ system of the body." One must however be careful with facile comparisons between a sudden event like nuclear attack as in Hiroshima and long-term trauma as in concentration camp life.

Psychosomatic conditions. Such conditions are quite common and form the basis for many German restitution claims. They can exhibit themselves immediately after liberation from the trauma or many years later. Research is needed to find out if there is a "ticking-clock" syndrome—illnesses induced by the Nazi experience 20, 30, or 40 years after the event. These conditions include diseases related to chronic states of tension or anger; gastrointestinal conditions, peptic ulcers, and related symptoms; cardiovascular disturbances such as angina pectoris, heart disease, etc.; cancer; and the typical survivor triad of headaches, persistent nightmares, and chronic depression accompanied by various psychosomatic complaints.

Psychotic and psychotic-like states. These occur in the most extreme cases of survivor traumata. Regressive and primitive methods of dealing with aggression can result in schizophrenic-like symptoms such as hallucinations, fantasy-building, states of depersonalization, hypochondriatic symptoms, or paranoid manifestations, all having a very specific history and determination.

Conclusion. Research in the field definitely shows that Holocaust survivors do manifest a psychological survivor syndrome with at minimum the survivor triad mentioned above, and at maximum, the more pathological problems stated above. It should be emphasized however that most survivors have adapted quite well to their traumatic experience and live fairly normal lives. Psychologists tend to generalize from small clinical samples and emphasize only the pathological. They should take a cue from Abraham Maslow and begin to balance the picture with case studies of the strengths and self-affirmations of Holocaust survivors. They too often dwell only on the negative. Research on the *positive* aspects of "survivorship" should be encouraged.

Coping Behavior of Survivors: Social and Political Adaptations

The study now moves away from psychological studies into the realm of sociology. Research on the sociology of Holocaust survivors and their children is almost non-existent. While there is some literature on the socio-political acculturation of immigrant groups to America, the following section is a first step towards a description of socio-political adaptation of specifically post-World War II Holocaust survivors. What follows is a brief series of observations and hypotheses that require more quantitative verification. The observations are generalized from the survivor community of Milwaukee, Wisconsin, where I lived from 1948-1968, and I discuss an Ashkenazic, Eastern European milieu. Other survivor communities, such as those composed of Sephardic or Austro-German Holocaust survivors, would differ in some respects from this sample in the areas of education, religiosity, assimilation, and other factors.

Jewish survivors of the Holocaust are also new immigrants to their host country, whether that be Israel, the USA, Canada, England, or Argentina. The burden of adapting to a new life-style, language, and culture is added to the already heavy burden of the Holocaust trauma. The kind of adjustment they make to their new homeland depends on many variables. Among these are family situation, maturity, age, level of education, job opportunities, religious background, support of relatives and social agencies, and support from within the community of survivors.

Despite all the difficulties, most survivors have adjusted quite well. Financially, they are fairly secure; some have even become quite wealthy in the short time they have been in America. Doing fairly well does not mean that in terms of occupational status and prestige, survivors have moved far up the social ladder, but they have done better than expected given generally low levels of education and training. Many of the Russian and Polish Jews of Milwaukee went into marginal trades; tailors, caterers, scrap metal or used auto parts dealers, mom and pop grocery stores, and garment industry jobs. A few became Hebrew teachers, cantors, sextons, and rabbis. Engineers, doctors, dentists, and professors are virtually non-existent in this community. German and Austrian Jews, on the other hand, because of their education and training, were more likely to be engaged in law, medicine, or other professions.

Like most American immigrants, survivors desired for their children the utmost in schooling, and for the most part they succeeded. Within a single generation, their children very nearly caught up occupationally and educationally with their host-country contemporaries. A great many survivor-children married non-survivor children and with their advanced training and education, they entered into professions such as teaching, social work, law, accounting, or business. A few joined their parents in the family business, a fact that their parents viewed as a step-down in prestige even though these same children are much better off financially than if they had gone into, for example, teaching.

Most parents expected their children to surpass them in education and occupational mobility, and though this caused some tension between generations, it was an accepted fact. Many survivor-parents sacrificed their lives for the sake of their children's careers. This kind of sacrifice is not new in American Jewish history. It occurred at the turn of the century during the great waves of immigration from Europe, and Jewish parents have been sacrificing ever since. It will be interesting to see whether the second generation of children will sacrifice for their children.

Survivor-parents of the Milwaukee Jewish community number about 1,000 out of a total of 24,000 Jews, and they tend to cluster around six synagogues, four of them Orthodox, on the northwest side of the city. Their children and even a growing number of the parents have moved to the east or northeast part of town, a more affluent section, yet they retain their ties to the "old" Jewish neighborhood.

While some parents may be non-observant, or even anti-observant, most continue to live in the religious community and observe traditions out of respect for the memory of their parents or because they truly believe in their Orthodox life-style. They know no other. The relationship to their rabbis—two of the *shuls* are led by Hasidic *rebbes*, is the same one they maintained in their *shetlach* and cities in Eastern Europe. As one rabbi told me: "I didn't leave Rovno; I brought it with me here and built an American Rovno in Milwaukee."

Politically, survivors tend to be somewhat passive and conservative. They keep a low profile, rarely becoming involved in city, state, or national politics. They try to avoid controversy, political or otherwise. Given their previous experiences, this conservatism is understandable. But another reason may simply be that they see themselves, even after thirty years in the country, as greenhorns. They are often ashamed of how they speak English, or how they act or dress. They feel that they are too ignorant of the political process to become involved, or that they will look foolish. Some are deeply suspicious and even mortally afraid of authority figures, whether policemen, politicians, or petty bureaucrats. Their children do not suffer from this fear.

Some survivors try to assimilate into the general Jewish community, and a tiny few into the general Christian population, but the vast majority seem most comfortable with their own kind. They feel that not only non-Jews but even other Jews do not really understand them or their past traumas. They react to their Americanized children in the same way. At times, neither the survivor nor the kin understands the other. Sometimes, the kin are ashamed of the survivor, and even feel the survivor is guilty for having survived.

In two areas, however, survivors are politically involved and their involvement comes with such force and devotion, that it sometimes shocks non-survivor Jews. These areas are the fate of Israel and the plight of Soviet Jewry. Survivors are very active in various fund-raising activities for these two causes, either within their synagogues or through survivor organizations such as the New American Club. These clubs should be studied more intensively. They form the nucleus of social activity for many survivors with their dances, raffles, and fund-raising events. These clubs are an opportunity for survivors to relax, speak Yiddish, and enjoy oneself in the company of a close-knit community of survivors. In fact, it is only at these clubs and at family events (weddings, bar mitzvot, a *bris*-circumcision) that I have seen survivors relax and temporarily forget their past traumas.

Their ties with Israel are extremely close, not only spiritually, but socially. Many survivors have relatives in Israel and there is much contact between them. Israel is crucial to survivors psychologically as one of the few havens for Jews anywhere in the world. A disproportionate number of them support militant pro-Israeli groups such as the Jewish Defense League or the Revisionist Zionists, though many are ambivalent about the violence associated with these two groups. Many survivors also join and support the Pioneer Women, Farband, and other Labor Zionist groups and if Orthodox, they will support the Mizrachi (Religious) Zionist organizations.

Survivors, like other Jews, have been staunch Democratic Party supporters from the time of President Truman. While there was some slippage toward the Republicans and to Richard Nixon in 1972, this was because Senator George McGovern, Nixon's opponent, was thought to have been soft in his support of Israel. In the future too, it seems that survivors will support those candidates that are firm in their defense of Israel regardless of the candidate's other positions.

Conclusions

There is much more that one could say about the sociology and politics of survivors. We can conclude that these survivors tend to live in tightly-knit survivor communities which consist of others who speak the same language, carry on the same customs of the Old Country, of the *shtetl* or the urban ghetto of Europe. They live a richly traditional but quiet life apart from other Jews in the community, and they donate much of their limited energies to their *shul*, their rabbi, Israeli causes, and the lives of their children and grandchildren. They work very hard, sometimes too hard, perhaps in order to try and forget the past. They are politically active and quite concerned, even paranoid, about anti-semitism and about Israel.

There is a socio-political "syndrome" that one can generalize. Survivors do share many common sociological features. Quotes around the word "syndrome" are used because the common dictionary meaning of the word is that of a complex or a group of traits that are abnormal and/or undesirable. The meaning of the term "syndrome" has been changed to include in this case a group of traits that are positive and normal; in other words, syndrome is used to mean any group of shared traits or features. In this sense, survivors do share a socio-political syndrome as well as a psychological one, and future studies must be social-psychological in the sense they begin to understand the survivor and the children *within* the context of, and not in isolation from, the community.

Coping Behavior of Survivor-Children: Psychological Adaptations

Who precisely is considered a child of survivors? Judith Kestenberg, an American psychiatrist who has done extensive research in this area, defines the child of survivors as "one who was born after the Holocaust or has not been himself subjected to persecution or maltreatment" (1972, p. 323). Though this definition is fine for now, a more complex one may be needed to also convey the impact of escape, migration, and childhood development in a family of survivors as well as the direct persecution by the Nazis. The subsequent post-war experience in DP camps can also lead to psychological conflicts. Kestenberg's definition is adequate even though it spreads over a large net of survivor-children, yet it technically leaves out those who *have* been subjected to persecution or maltreatment. I suppose these children could then be considered both survivors *and* children of survivors. In any case, Kestenberg's definition will prove adequate for this discussion.

In the past few years, there has been an increased interest in the children of survivors by psychologists and by the children themselves. One should really call them young adults rather than children because most of them are now between 20 and 35 years old and are at an age where they are forming groups of survivors' children in order to discuss the implications of their self-identity. A few years ago there was not a great deal of data on the subject except for several symposia and scattered articles, all of them emphasizing the psychoanalytical impact. However, the children of survivors themselves have begun to write about their experiences and have initiated research on the topic. Much of the earlier psychiatric literature is sketchy and has small clinical samples. Also, the non-psychiatric writings are impressionistic. However, new research should soon reveal if a psychological syndrome exists among the offspring of survivors and what its parameters are. It seems, however, that with some pathological exceptions, there appears to be a mild syndrome in the making; nothing that should alarm people, but enough of a syndrome to study and evaluate.

Kestenberg herself believed (in 1972) that there was no specific syndrome among children of survivors but she was cautious about closing the book on the subject. A rather bizarre and exceptional case had forced her to keep the question open:

> Some years ago I analyzed a young adolescent who behaved in a bizarre way, starving himself, hiding in woods and treating me. . .as a hostile persecutor. Soon after I connected his psychotic-like behavior with the real experiences of his parents' relatives in Europe, his symptoms abated but his analysis had to be prematurely terminated, chiefly because of his parental resistance. Haunted by the image of this patient, who came to me emaciated and hollow-eyed like a Musselman in a concentration camp, I looked at children of survivors in Israel and thought I could recognize in some faces a far away look, reminiscent of the stare of survivors of persecution. (1972, pp. 311-312)

A conclusion reached by Kestenberg was that psychiatrists themselves resisted unearthing the frightening impact of Nazi persecution on these young people. This fear appears to have abated in the past few years as more therapists are becoming aware of the need of these children to talk about their experiences.

A large number of survivors' children have sought psychiatric treatment for general problems but few therapists discuss the Holocaust as an important aspect of the child's socialization process, even though it often is an important factor.

Therapy can be of great help not only in relieving the stress of emotional conflicts but more importantly in accelerating communication between parents and child. As one child comments:

> My parents never told me anything about the war. . . . It was like sex. You didn't talk about it in my house. . . The house was like a tomb. Sometimes we went on picnics together. But underneath something was missing. (Mostysser, 1975, pp. 4-5)

What was missing was emotional contact between the generations and a deeper, cathartic sharing of the parent's fate and its effect on them as well as upon their children. Too often parents were too ashamed or afraid to discuss the subject with their offspring. They did not wish to burden their children with their suffering and their stories. Yet the child could sense the parents' suffering while not understanding its root in the other. At times children would blame themselves for their parents' suffering and a complex web of sadness, guilt, and helplessness would develop. Happily, more and more parents are talking to their children today. The NBC Holocaust TV special helped and the children themselves are older and more mature, more capable of initiating discussion of this formerly taboo subject. As one son of survivors recently told me: "After the NBC special, now everyone knows what I mean when I say that my parents went through the Holocaust. Everyone can share the burden a little bit, a burden that I have carried alone for over 30 years."

Eva Fogelman, a New York psychologist and a daughter of survivors, has been quoted as saying:

> I saw that psychiatrists were beginning to extend the Survivor Syndrome to us, that severe pathology was being attributed to the second generation just as it had been to our parents . . . I began to feel that this was all wrong. Sure we were effected. But not to the point where we're not functioning normally or where we have more psychological problems than the normal population. (Epstein, 1977, p. 14)

Ms. Fogelman and her colleague Bella Savran began to run "awareness groups" for children of survivors in the spring of 1976, similar to women's consciousness-raising groups, or better yet, like rap-groups for Vietnam veterans. I would agree with Fogelman and Savran (1979) that a pathological secondary syndrome does not appear to exist, but a milder guilt syndrome may be a possibility. Robert Lifton calls this syndrome the "death imprint." Children may feel ashamed of their parent's victimization. This shame in turn can often lead to a series of conflicts within the child, between parent and child, and between the child and the outside world.

Steven Greenblatt (1978), in a study of ten children of Nazi concentration camp survivors, half of whom were engaged in some form of psychotherapy, with the other half having no such treatment, found that the clinical group expressed a great deal more emotional turmoil, were more frequently exposed to Holocaust material than the non-clinical group, and had stronger feelings of inherited attitudes, most notably more survival guilt feelings due to unresolved grief reaction, inadequate coping mechanisms, and subsequent crises proneness. One could question both the size and the reliability/validity of the sample, but it is one of a growing number of studies that is finding some kind of secondary syndrome at work.

Often the parents are so preoccupied with the unending mourning process and the problems of starting a new life in a strange country that they are unable to relate to their children's needs or respond with the necessary flexibility. The children's demands become overwhelming and are seen by parents as draining their already limited emotional resources. The parents then attack their children for not listening and for not understanding them. Often it is difficult to tell who is the child and who is the adult in these cases. Because they are unable to cope with the continuous anxious responses of their parents to their behavior, the children may either go out of control or respond by withdrawal into fantasy at best, or into an affectless state at worse (Sigal, 1971, pp. 58-59).

What are the effects on the survivor's children, if their parents raised them with few controls and with over-permissiveness, since because they had suffered so much, they could not tolerate their children being deprived in any way? If one has lost everything in the Holocaust, a parent may take no chances in making this "special" survivor-child unhappy. It fits the typical Yiddishah Mamma, but the survivor-parent may greatly exaggerate the usual overprotectiveness of the Jewish mother. There can appear some minor forms of sado-masochism as well, with their roots in an ambivalence toward parents. They both love and are disgusted by their parents for many reasons: (a) for not being "American" or "modern" enough, and thus being ashamed of their parents; (b) seeing their parents as weak and passive before the Nazis, and thus coming into conflict with the usual image of a strong, powerful parent; (c) blaming their parents for their suffering and misery, thus setting up a round of guilt and anger and then more guilt.

Another component of a syndrome, if a syndrome does in fact exist, is the child's behavior toward authority figures, including parents, and subsequent feelings of guilt which anger and aggression toward these figures provoke. The child who has violent urges of aggression is confronted with a paradox, and either consciously or unconsciously says: "How can I attack someone who has already suffered so much?" Parents and child then turn on each other, each escalating the other's feelings of guilt. Each blames the other for their mutual sense of deprivation and frustration. A lack of communication, a blurred sense of identity, and a potential for depression can result from the dynamics of this game of guilt (Sigal, 1971, p. 59).

All of this still leaves open the question of whether there is a psychological syndrome among the children of survivors. Nevertheless, any syndrome theory will have to take into account the following variables:

Age. There is some impressionable data that the first child born after the war may suffer more intensely from the secondary guilt syndrome than other siblings and that all the conflicts mentioned earlier may affect him or her more than later children. The first-born child is a special child to the parents, with much promise and responsibility. It represents the rebirth of the family and the resurrection of earlier children killed by the Nazis. While the first-born may carry extra burdens, it may also be far more ambitious, successful, and creative precisely because it has been imbued with the special hopes and needs of the parents. The child may have messianic ambitions. Children born subsequently may suffer less than the first-born, but may also achieve less.

Time of birth. An important variable may be when and where the child was born; whether in the death camps, in the forests, the ghetto, the DP (displaced person) camp after the war, or later, in the host country.

Post-Holocaust experiences. These experiences are often overlooked in analysis but can prove crucial. The shock of the European liberation, the displacement from previous homes, the escape from Communist countries, the trip to the host country, the formation of new families or of families re-uniting, and adjustment to the hardships of the new country are all crucial components in any syndrome theory. The post-Holocaust phase is rarely mentioned in the literature yet can be as traumatic to survivors and their children as was the actual war-time experience.

Time of departure. Did the survivors leave before or after the war? Many German and Austrian Jews were able to leave Germany in the mid to late 1930s. Was their trauma different from the Russian or Polish Jews who managed to survive the war?

Emotional stability of parents. All persons suffered severe personal trauma during the war. The level of emotional maturity before and during the war is important in understanding to what extent the Holocaust affected parents and their children. The intactness of the family is also important. If there was a loss of a spouse, survivors tended to remarry as soon as possible after the war. These dyadic relationships were very strong even if romance or deep love was missing; often these were marriages of convenience. All these factors can affect the children.

Reaction to new stress. Adaptation after persecution is of course the key element to understanding the impact of Holocaust experiences on the children. The need to succeed and the need to work to help forget the past can lead to a tendency for over-achievement and over-involvement whether in school, business, or politics, among the children of survivors. This will be discussed in the next section.

Participation in wars of liberation. Active participation in either the regular army, the World War II resistance movements, or the Israeli wars seems to have had a beneficial effect on both survivors and their children. The channeling of feelings of powerlessness and worthlessness against a common enemy, whether Nazis or Arabs, was beneficial for mental health. The ability to take revenge was also satisfying, though never totally, since no amount of revenge could replace the loss experienced. If a parent could not fight, then vigorous support for Israel and/or for militant Jewish groups such as the JDL would suffice vicariously. Whether the parent resisted or simply hid in a cave during the war may have an important impact on the children of survivors in the sense that a socio-political response could develop as a result; i.e. joining the JDL or some leftist radical group as a form of continuity in resisting anti-Semitism and racism.

Conclusions

Quite likely a minor secondary guilt syndrome among the children of survivors will be found but it is too early, given the data, to say for sure. Even so, it will be mild compared to the parents. If left to the psychiatrists, they will frighten us with predictions of a severe, pathologicial second-generation survivor's syndrome. I do not believe that a pathology exists, and if there is a syndrome, it will be benign. A balance of the psychiatric side of the coin with sociological analyses is necessary. Such analyses will present the positive and creative side of being a child of survivors and balance the negative. Furthermore, larger samples, at least 50-100 offspring of survivors, are needed in order to generalize about all children of survivors. Without these large samples, an incomplete picture of the situation will emerge.

Coping Behavior of Survivor Children: Social and Political Adaptations

Several writers (Robert J. Lifton, Viktor Frankl, Michael Barkun) have noticed that the Holocaust, whether of Hiroshima or of Auschwitz, has imposed a sense of confusion and unspeakable horror. While some have been psychically numbed, to use Lifton's phrase, others have attempted to remake the world. Being a survivor can lead either to silence or to chivalry. The children of survivors have discovered that they must make some sense out of the Holocaust, to give this awesome and meaningless mass death some meaning. Their responses have often been creative.

According to Helen Epstein (1977, p. 14), children of survivors are quite diverse. They range in age from late teens to middle-thirties and include housewives, students, teachers, business people, artists, social workers, doctors, and others. They are single, married, divorced, homosexual, and heterosexual. They include strictly Orthodox and anti-religious Jews. Their political affiliations are radical, liberal, conservative, Zionist, anti-Zionist, or apolitical. They live in the cities or in the country. Some say that their parents' experience has affected them only slightly while others say that it has determined their choice of profession, friends, and spouses.

Yet despite their diversity, Epstein maintains that there is a sense of affinity among children of survivors, or as one put it: "There is a tacit understanding between us;" "A completeness without conversation," as another said. It is this affinity that has brought children of survivors together into groups with names like "One Generation After."

Is there a socio-political "syndrome" among the children of survivors? Are there distinct socio-political responses to the Holocaust, if not from all children, then from large segments of them? If there is a syndrome of some kind, and it is too early to say as of now because of lack of research, then it will consist of two major components, each component containing two parts—(1) Particularistic (or Jewish involvement): (a) Religious; (b) Political, and—(2) Universalistic (or beyond the Jewish realm): (a) Religious; (b) Political.

Let us first examine some examples of the particularisticly Jewish ways of confronting the Holocaust. A good number of survivor-children are involved in some form of Jewish commitment. This commitment is based on the idea that young Jews feel they must not give Hitler a posthumous "victory;" that is, they must not assimilate and disappear as Jews, thus giving Hitler his ultimate triumph—the annihilation of the Jewish people. These young Jews become survivalists, and in defiance of anti-Semitic abuse, they emerge as "new" Jews, fighting-proud Jews. Religiously, this can lead to Orthodox or Hasidic life-styles; politically to a variety of expressions ranging from a tough chauvinistic stance like the Jewish Defense League or the right-wing Revisionist Zionist position of youth groups like Betar, to a tough socialist, leftist position.

It can include being Jewish activists; being involved in the rights of Soviet Jews; editing Jewish magazines; organizing religious communal groups; and other similar pursuits. Israel becomes important as the visible continuity of Jewish survival. These interests are of course effected by similar parental political activity and by

Jewish education in Hebrew schools, but can also emerge from other sources; the direct immersion in Holocaust literature, a visit to Israel and its Holocaust centers (Yad Vashem or Kibbutz Yad Mordechai, for example), or a particular writer or teacher, such as Elie Weisel or Emil Fackenheim. In the past ten years, whenever Israel was threatened, the nightmare of another Holocaust re-appeared and this too has led to increased political activity on the part of Holocaust survivors and their children.

In the universalistic setting beyond the Jewish realm, young Jews would see in the Holocaust a motif for present-day political concerns—nuclear Holocaust, the Vietnam war, racism, air and water pollution, and violence. Jewish universalists have found a Jewish setting for their activities too narrow and confining. Therefore, they would go beyond Judaism to embrace other elements. Religiously, this could include a millenial religious movement or cult in which they could work not only for the salvation of the Jews but for all people. It would be interesting to find out how many children of survivors have joined such cults. In all likelihood the number is small because such a non-Jewish cult would be a negation of their Jewish identity which the Holocaust etched so sharply, yet some young Jews would opt for this alternative despite the anguished reaction of parents and friends.

More likely, Holocaust survivor-children will be involved in universal *political* movements, either radical groups such as socialist or Marxist sects or liberal groups working in the area of human rights, ecology, nuclear energy, and race relations. The image of the Holocaust is powerful and while not the only factor, it is an important one in understanding why and how some children react to their parents' experience by joining radical or liberal political movements.

Is There a Survivor Syndrome? A Conclusion of Sorts

What can be said in summary? First, with regard to the presence of a psychological survivor syndrome among first generation parents of the Holocaust, the evidence for its existence is overwhelming. The works of Winnik, Krystal, Neiderland and others, plus the compendium of literature on the subject in Krystal & Niederland, (1971) confirms this conclusion. It should be emphasized that most survivors have adapted to their trauma quite well, and more stress should be placed on the positive side of this adaptation. Furthermore, more research is needed on the social psychology and the sociology of survivors and of survivor communities in the world. Too often, psychiatrists have emphasized the pathological and they have done so using clinical samples that are too small and unrepresentative of the range of adaptations and coping mechanisms that survivors utilize.

As for a socio-political syndrome, the evidence shows that there does appear to be a constellation of adaptive mechanisms at work—conservatism, traditionalism, political paranoia, concern for Israel, but more research is needed to confirm the range of this syndrome politically, sociologically, and religiously.

As for the children of survivors, there exist some problems with generalizations. Some scholars feel that it is too early to report about the exact specificity of a psychological syndrome or its absence (Kestenberg, 1972). A good deal of research is being undertaken now and some reliable answers should be available soon. There is a basis for a secondary guilt syndrome emerging in the children of survivors; a second-generation syndrome may emerge. It will likely be mild in its psycho-pathological aspects, but there will be some exceptions, as Kestenberg herself discovered. One should not exaggerate the severity of such a syndrome; most children of survivors are the normal everyday neurotics that one finds among any highly educated group.

Regarding a socio-political syndrome among the children of survivors, again there may well be not just one syndrome or constellation of responses, but several kinds, either religious or political and either universal or particular. The offspring of Holocaust survivors have to mold some kind of response and find some form of meaning to their experience, and this can lead to a fascinating and diverse set of reactions. Naturally, the Holocaust is not the only independent variable affecting one's social, political, or religious life. Other variables such as one's secular and religious education, childhood relationships with parents, political and cultural socialization, the politics of one's parents, and related factors, aside from the Holocaust, are clearly crucial. What is certain is that a small but significant number of the children of survivors have a fascination for revolutionary, radical, or millenial movements and this fact in itself is a significant observation worthy of future research. (See Figure 1.)

The cycle continues. The second generation is getting married and having children. Some of these children are already in their early teens. Most of the third generation of survivors' (grand) children are young. It is still too early to predict about a syndrome on their part. There should be no psychological syndrome of any consequences unless the parents have serious psychological problems directly related to *their* parents' Holocaust experience. But as for a socio-political syndrome, it

	Psychological Syndrome	Socio-Political Syndrome a) Religious b) Political
1st Generation (parents)	Yes	a) Yes b) Yes
2nd Generation (children)	Possibly, but mild (with some exceptions)	a) Possibly b) Possibly
3rd Generation (grandchildren)	No (with some exceptions)	A distinct posibility

FIGURE 1. Survival Syndromes

would not be surprising if particular traditions related to the Holocaust are passed on to future generations. Just as the Daughters of the American Revolution continue to adhere to a tradition many generations later, so too there may well be socio-political and religious responses specifically developed by the offspring of survivors, trailing far into the future.

References

Epstein, H. The heirs of the holocaust. *The New York Times Magazine,* June 19, 1977, 12-15; 74-77.
Greenblatt, S. The influence of survival guilt in chronic family crises. *Journal of Psychology and Judaism, 1978, 2*(2), 19-28.
Grosser, G., Welchsler, H., & Greenblatt, M. (Eds.). *The threat of impending disaster: Contributions to the psychology of distress.* Cambridge, Mass.: MIT Press, 1964.
Kestenberg, J. Psychoanalytic contributions to the problem of children of survivors from Nazi persecutions. *Israel Annals of Psychiatry and Related Disciplines,* 1972, *10*(4), 311-325.
Krystal, H. & Niederland, W. (Eds.). *Psychic traumatization.* Boston: Little, Brown, 1971.
Mostysser, T. Children of survivors: Growing up in America with a holocaust heritage. *Martyrdom and Resistance,* 1975, *1*(6), 4-5.
Fogelman, E. & Savran, B. Therapeutic groups for children of holocaust survivors. *International Journal of Group Psychotherapy,* 1979, *29*(2), 211-236.
Sigal, J. Second-generation effects of massive psychic trauma. In H. Krystal & Niederland (Eds.), *Psychic traumatization.* Boston: Little, Brown, 1971.

Second Generation Effects of the Holocaust: The Effectiveness of Group Therapy in the Resolution of the Transmission of Parental Trauma

FLORABEL KINSLER received her Masters in Social Work from the School of Social Welfare at the University of California at Los Angeles and is presently a clinical social worker with the Jewish Family Service of Los Angeles. She has also served as medical social work consultant. She is on the field work faculty of the University of Southern California and Hebrew Union College, maintains a private practice, and has delivered papers and authored works on holocaust survivors, children of holocaust survivors, and counter-transference issues with this segment of the population.

ABSTRACT: The importance of sensitizing therapists to the special needs of clients whose parents experienced profound long-term, wartime trauma is discussed. The discussion relates to the Holocaust of the Jews during the Second World War, but broader implications, albeit lesser, exist for other peoples caught up in terror and cruelty, such as the refugees who preceded them in the late 1930's. Evidence exists to support the hypothesis that transference and countertransference issues relating to survivor guilt in the client and in the therapist have not been sufficiently recognized. The transmission of violence and evil, unwittingly, from one generation to another is elaborated upon, and attention is given to the short-term group treatment approaches utilized at the Jewish Family Service of Los Angeles to bring awareness to the children of survivors.

Children of survivors, estimated at 125,000-150,000 in North America, have now matured and are motivated for their own therapy. Struggling with ambivalence to emancipate from often painfully injured parents, they seek their own psychic answers in increasing numbers. Well they might, since the parents frequently aborted the therapy sought as they raised them. Perhaps threatened, having little hope for the future, counseling was rejected as useless. It was as though, abandoned by the world in their years of torment and captivity, the parents could not and would not permit themselves to believe that their situations were salvageable by anyone but themselves. Thus trust issues underlie this hopelessness along with questions of worthiness; did they really deserve service? Further, parents often feel shame when their child reflects their own imperfections; the narcissistic hurts which result from a child's attempt to individuate and emancipate. It is especially difficult when the child unconsciously represents the resurrection of the parents' own near deaths and the deaths of others in the family.

It is essential to underline the considerable achievements and adequacy of large numbers of children of survivors. However, when troubled, the following complex is noticeable.

Children of Survivor Complex

Among the characteristic difficulties are:

1. The separation-individuation vs. fusion with parents and siblings. The ensuing struggles over autonomy have led to feelings of anger and guilt. The danger of merger exists, balanced precariously against the risk that these parents will experience emancipation as yet another abandonment.
2. Narcissistic injuries. Good early bonding and mirroring, in Kohut's (1978) terms, existed where the parents had sufficient affect to cathect to the children. However, at the separation-individuation stage the parent might have felt rejected and victimized. At this point insufficient mirroring would have resulted. Along the "Grandiose Self-Scale" of development, again, a good start may have been made. However, at an oedipal level, the demeaning of one parent by the other would have had a negative effect on the "Idealized Imago."
3. A damaged sense of self. Children of survivors have felt that their lives, successes, and failures are not their own. They have had little validation for their feelings, instead hearing from the parents that their troubles could not compare with the parents' experiences. They have felt their lives to have less meaning. The reaction formation here may lead to overachievement or giving up and dropping out. Paradoxically, they have felt like replacements for lost relatives, and they have needed to achieve to absolve parents of their shame.

4. Poor impulse control, leading to antisocial acts, such as stealing, "getting away with" behavior, impatience, drug abuse. Some of this may be seen as pseudo-psychopathy and possibly reversible, as in the borderline conditions. The "acting out" may be a release of intolerable tension. Other aspects of this are clearly sociopathic.
5. Rage-related dynamics, violence to the self and others, depression with some suicide attempts, sado-masochistic behavior.
6. Impairment in forming intimate interpersonal relationships and work relationships. Frequency of divorce is noted and several have decided not to have children.
7. Psychosis.

Although these symptoms alone are not unusual, it is the intensity and frequency with which they appear that seems to form an identifiable and recognizable complex.

Research

Considerable research continues on children of survivors, both in North America and Israel, with preponderantly clinical populations. Hospitalized children of survivors have been reported by Dr. Sylvia Axelrod (1978).

Three major psychiatric conferences have been reported on the subject. Additionally, I have derived, from Sonnenberg's report (1971), the following:

1. Involved in the survivors' anxiety is a wish to avoid pain in their children.
2. A resurrection fantasy exists in the survivor in which the child is identified with the parent's exterminated sibling and forced into a pre-existing mold that hampers maturation.
3. Anger resulting from the parents' feelings of abandonment is somehow communicated to the children.
4. Adolescent delinquency is the result of parental closeness. Further, the report mentions that parental superego deficits resulting from concentration camp experiences are transmittable to the children.

Oftentimes, the parents have taught them from their own behavior how to deal with and beat the system as if to elevate the self-esteem and as a protective device. On the other hand, one hears of parents who are intimidated by authority.

Sonnenberg points also to exaggerated ethnic identity as an undoing of the humiliation of the camps and adds that the societal rejection and narcissistic humiliation of the parents has been conveyed to the children regarding their Jewishness.

He further reports discussion of difficulty with ego identifications, splitting, ideals, impediments to oedipal resolution, and acting out in both the parents and children.

Suffice to say that affecting the quality of what some survivors had to offer their children were the following: preoccupation due to incomplete mourning, guilt and fear of enjoying too much to avoid tempting fate (jinxing), and again losing the loved object. There is evidence that distancing behavior is prevalent. Survivor families frequently do not speak to their few surviving relatives for one reason or another. It would seem that accepting human foibles is more than survivor fantasies and hopes for reunion can tolerate. All of this leads to ambivalent messages and inconsistent behavior. Where self-images were sufficiently damaged, their decision-making processes have also been affected, leading to anxiety projected through overprotection.

It is important to note that a vast nonclinical population exists. Indeed, some survivors successfully navigated the perilous waters of parenting through the upheavals of the 1960s and 1970s, drugs and all, with sufficient pleasure and constancy to produce assertive, sound, and maturing families.

Diverse Views

Though this study relies heavily upon the reports of the Wayne State Conference (1964), the International Congress of Child Psychiatry Jerusalem Conference (1970), the writings of Hoppe (1969), Krystal (1968), Niederland (1968), Lifton (1976), etc., in forming and supporting the thinking, symptomatically and diagnostically, about survivors and their families, it is important to note that divergent views exist.

Isaac Kanter (1976) makes a case against the use of Freudian conceptualizations that omit the understanding of ethnic identity and cultural heritage. He differentiates the ethnic-conscious Jew from the assimilated Jew, the German Jew from the Polish Jew, and the pre-war Zionist as having distinguishing characteristics that affected their responses to the persecutions.

Regarding the Jerusalem Conference, Sigal (1977) states that the search for hypotheses of the effects of survivors of the holocaust on the psychological functioning of their children resulted in unclear findings. Sigal later discussed a Canadian experiment regarding the "preoccupation hypothesis," in which consequences similar to those experienced by children of survivors were noted in the clinical population of "non-survivors." These people were preoccupied for other reasons, i.e., alcoholism, etc. He states that although there are consistent patterns in the families studied clinically, they must not be considered as unique nor as homogeneous. Despite that, he found the reports productive in treatment recommendations.

Countertransference Issues and Survivor Guilt

Countertransference problems exist among competent and well-meaning therapists. This is attested to by Judith Kestenberg's (1973) worldwide poll of psycholanalysts and by Hoppe (1969), quoting Eissler. A possible factor is the resistance that the survivor parents and the children themselves have to exploring the influence of the Nazi persecution upon their lives. Contributing to this implicit "conspiracy" was an attitude widely held by other professionals following World War II, which considered the survivors untreatable due to their massive traumatization. Uncovering of traumata was feared to be risking psychotic breakdown by overwhelming the client with long-repressed material. This attitude continues, and I concur with Bertha Simos' (1979) recent warnings that therapeutic interventions be cautiously entered upon. However, it is important that this caution be flexibly applied. Further, overcaution should not be transmitted so that the treatment of the children is overly delineated. Therapists must be alerted to the potential for rejecting the children of survivors during treatment on these bases. Some therapists may evidence an overidentification with the child-of-survivor client and attempt to make restitution for parental deficits. The "non-survivor" therapist may react as apologist for the noncaring world of the 1940s, infecting the treatment with guilt. The survivor therapist and child of survivor therapist are in danger of overidentification. As with any population, therapists must be sensitive to any countertransference phenomena within themselves that might lead to distortion of the therapeutic process (Kinsler, 1980, Pomerantz, 1980).

Contacts with survivors have at times left agency social workers rejected and negated. Survivors have had to respond with disdain when confronting a reality that is less than they had hoped for. Once again, they feel disappointment. Further, there is the distance created by the vastness of what they have known and experienced. This distance is made greater by the therapist's shame and fearfulness, knowing what survivors have endured. The shame relates to the "shadow," in Jungian terms, which taps in on the repressed fantasies of cruelty, the darkness within all of us. Researchers relate that an additional hindrance to the therapeutic process may arise out of the therapist's fear of contamination by the evil exposed in working with the survivor family.

The phenomenon of survivor guilt may be more widely experienced than formerly realized. For some, it was not until the publication of Anne Frank's experience that they became aware of their own vulnerability, and the good fortune associated with the location of their birth.

Through World War II, many second and third generation American Jews had little or no identification with European or Israeli Jewry. What was observable was a callousness of many to the "refugee" of the 1930s. There existed an insensitivity and misunderstanding by the depression-rent American Jew of the "arrogance" of the elite Berliner or Viennese. What was not understood was that these claims to the greatness of the former life in Germany or Austria was a twisting of the grief, an expression of the inner rage over the betrayal and loss of the homeland. The rescuers had expected gratitude and loyalty, but the "refugees" had been outcast, stripped of identity. How and whom could they trust but their past? The rescuers had choice in their role, the "refugees" had not.

Another therapeutic complication arose when the "survivor"cum "displaced person" arrived on our shores at the end of World War II. They were expected to embrace life when they were only recently resurrected from a death-like condition, in which they had repeatedly given up their lives in certainty of death. Ernest Becker analyzes the brilliant film characterization of the "Pawnbroker" (1969) as it exemplified the survivor's inability to lay down the "character armor." The resulting response to the professional "helping" person was laced with rage and projected despair. Often, this was more than social workers could bear. I speculate that the grieving process was cut short out of our own survivor guilt and caused survivors to close off with denial and to ghettoize their feelings.

Transference Issues

In addition to distrust, distance and shame, already touched upon, survivors transferred to the social workers, physicians, and psychiatric staff all manner of negative responses to authority figures. Still involved is the role in which they first knew a social worker, as an intermediary for "the agency," remembering the insensitivities that were unwittingly displayed to their felt needs as these needs interfered with agency realities and policies. This followed soon after their dealings with the authorities of the DP camps, preceded by the horrendous repetitive cruelties of the underlings of the large repressive systems they had known in captivity.

What, then, of their envy of the professional's lives, educations, family, and their fantasies of what might have been possible for themselves, the dreams interrupted by the war?

Treatment Issues

For several years it was not recognized that a growing number of children of survivors were presenting themselves for therapy. These were the tots resettled almost twenty years before with their parents. Caseworkers listened to them, recognized similar patterns associated with the parents' trauma, learned from them, reflected back, interpreted and confronted. Above all, it was necessary to judiciously give hope for change, to infuse optimism where pessimism prevailed. It was essential to relate to their late adolescent and young adult pain, their struggle with uncertainties about themselves and about their careers. Their concerns included involved relationships with their parents, characterized by excessive ambivalence. These young adults were thrust, still unemancipated, from the double bind of European and religious standards foreign to a swift-moving American mainstream.

At first, the treatment approaches were the conservative tools of our trade, i.e., family and individual therapy, with little professional recognition of a growing phenomenon. In 1972 the potential for group therapy as an intervention was recognized. However, never at one time was sufficient population available. It was necessary to sensitize the agency staff to these concerns.

The subject of using groups met considerable professional resistance in Los Angeles. Several respected figures in the social work and psychiatric community held serious reservations concerning homogeneous groups and brief treatment for this population. Others were more supportive.

We started, therefore, with reservations, and our concerns about going public proved warranted. Some survivors among the staff, colleagues, and among the parents were resistive and seemed threatened by the intent. Parents of group members have frequently questioned the purpose. Some members have defined the groups as "classes" to calm parental qualms.

The initial choice of the group method was affected by three concerns. We were aware that:

1. The subject and material be presented to the community in such a way as to minimize stigmatizing this population and their parents;
2. Long-repressed material might overwhelm poorly-defended clients;
3. The material discussed might be used by certain group members as a rationalization for any or all personal discomforts, a greater risk in a homogeneous group.

As a result of these issues, we first decided upon a discussion or rap group format, borrowing heavily from Family Life Education. By February of 1978 we instituted brief group therapy, and in September 1979, a heterogeneous group was begun.

Thirteen groups have been run, one was aborted and we are accumulating individuals for a fourteenth.

The Discussion Groups

This format uses semieducational techniques to realize the goal of preventative mental health. We utilized an outreach approach by advertising in the local Jewish press, contacting local universities, synagogues, former clients and colleagues. The screening process included a telephone interview, during which we attempted to determine the client's motivation and appropriateness for the group, their perceptions about the subject, and their questions. It is esential that a firm commitment for all sessions be required and exclude acquaintances to minimize resistances. The initial group was comprised of 12 individuals ranging in age from 23 to 31. The group members were predominantly well-functioning individuals in a variety of professional, semiprofessional, and business positions, as well as graduate students. In another instance a member had a manic-depressive psychosis with repeated hospitalizations and was controlled by Lithium and therapy. There have been prison involvements resulting from violent behavior to the self or others in three group members. Most members of the groups had at least one parent who had experienced the concentration camps or years of concealment in occupied territory. A $25.00 fee for the eight sessions was set with partial scholarships available, as had been the custom with Family Life Education groups in the past.

The co-therapists, one of whom was a child of survivors, proceeded with self-introductions and agenda gathering. Agreement was reached on one or two foci for the discussion of that evening. Presentation of relevant material, including concurrent world events brought by the members was encouraged and, at times, offered by the leaders. Information from a "life cycle" perspective was introduced. The therapists and clients entered with an attitude of pioneering, to assess the validity for such groups by eliciting their interest and feedback. At the outset we were still unaware of the existence of groups in other parts of the country and proceeded cautiously. Our intent was to draw as much experience, information, and feeling from the members as possible, while avoiding excessive affect stimulation in keeping with the tenets of a preventative program and the Family Life Education model.

Brief Therapy Groups

As a result of our encouraging experience in the first group and the newly available experience of Savran and Fogelman (1979) in Boston, regarding their brief therapy model, with a similar population, we decided to extend and seek affect-laden material in a short-term therapy group. This ran concurrently with a second discussion group. Prospective members then had a choice of discussion or therapy groups. A fee more commensurate with group therapy was set, $10.00 per session, and now $20.00. Again, scholarships were readily available. In addition to the phone interview, the co-therapists now interviewed each prospective participant in order to assess their ego strength, motivation, self-awareness, and suitability for short-term therapy. This interview offered them the opportunity to assess us and our comfort with the Holocaust-related material, a concern of many who had found therapists unwilling to deal with the material. Where other individuals were involved in other therapy, permission from those therapists was obtained. We informed each participant that we and the agency would be available for therapeutic services beyond the confines of the group for those not already in treatment. In succeeding groups, other staff members have been encouraged to join each of the original teams as co-therapists, propagating interest and developing skill with this population. Our use of leaders who are survivors, children of survivors, and general population have all been well met.

The latter was a surprising finding, as was the rapid development of cohesion during the first and second sessions, common to both groups' methodologies. The participants quickly identified with each other's experiences. It was as if they were inside each other's skins. With this sharing of data an empathic resonance ensued (Kohut & Wolf, 1978). In almost all of the groups a warm, sensitive, and protective atmosphere flourished. Confrontations were generally handled in a supportive manner, although there has been divisiveness. Direct, painful verbal assaults have occurred with productive working through in the therapy groups. In one instance it was necessary to debrief group members individually at termination because of concerns regarding one member's behavior. In the Family Life Education format the therapists were more active in controlling group discussion, process, and affect, whereas, in the therapy groups, the reins have largely been in the group's hands to enhance process.

Survey of Response to Groups

The participants' response to the groups has, thus far, been highly encouraging. More than half of the clients responded to our questionnaires with a very high percentage positively. They have noted that feelings, once secret and alienating, have been validated by their group experience, resulting in considerable emotional relief. Additionally, they stated that the group discussion helped them feel more understanding, accepting, and forgiving of their parents. This is characterized by a decrease in defensiveness and an increased ability to understand the meaning of the parents' behavior and response as separate from themselves. Several indicated greater comfort with their Jewishness and feeling more a part of the Jewish community. At least one person felt relieved to learn of the accessibility of the agency's services to her parents. It is my feeling that the therapy groups will not develop the degree of closure regarding the relationships and forgiveness of parents as the discussion groups. This should not be considered a negative value judgment, since a more significant working through may occur with the passage of longer periods of time following the brief therapy or in longer-term therapy.

Relevant Issues

There have been several common issues discussed in the groups thus far. The universal struggle common to almost all was for autonomy and a sense of self. We heard complaints of parental overinvolvement in their lives. At other times there was evidence that the group member was unconsciously inviting the parents' continued participation, as if to maintain the situation, i.e., choosing to be dependent financially upon the parents, manipulative so that auto registration was in the parents' name, using the parents to babysit while critical of their performance.

There was an almost universal denial of shame. This belies considerable evidence of undoing, overachieving and overcompensating. We wondered whether some of the daring escapades alluded to might have been stimulated by this.

Some participants compared themselves to their parents, wondering whether they could have survived the horrors of the camps, expressing pride in their parents, but suffering by comparison. This often resulted in a sense that their lives and experiences were somehow less significant than those of their parents.

Paradoxically, they reported feeling their lives to be extremely important. In truth, the parents' ability to conceive in the Displaced Persons camps was, after earlier losses of secondary sexual characteristics, i.e., cessation of menses in the camps, something of a miracle. They felt burdened to make up for their parents' suffering and multiple losses. The sense of "specialness," being unique, "the chosen people," was for some a part of this theme. These are apparent distortions of narcissism to be struggled with.

I have observed the additional stress on the first-born, or only child born into the grieving process. Such a child also serves as a transitional object. These children have talked of conducting much of the family business affairs, explaining forms and dealing with the authorities for their parents since early childhood. Often, they were the first to speak English and carried new customs into the home. This was in the tradition of immigrant families. The difference lay in the mood and condition of the parents, their willingness or lack of interest and enthusiasm for new experiences. Later siblings seem to have been less affected. It seems likely that the passage of time has eased some of the trauma.

Another emerging group theme was the sense of joylessness or a feeling that one had no right to be happy because of the parents' losses and continued grieving. They asked each other whether their homes contained pictures, music; whether the parents took vacations?

Many members have described angry feelings that they have towards their parents. They have noted that often their parents would not be emotionally available to them, sometimes preoccupied. The parents would deny them the right to experience their own pain, with comments such as "what are you crying about, you don't know what it means to suffer," which served to invalidate them and produced rage. On the other hand, they talked about receiving material gifts, i.e., food, money, which they viewed with a sense of irony as stereotypically manipulative.

A discussion of guilt regularly arose. It is considered by some members as a "Jewish disease." They see guilt resulting from many sources; rebellion, separation, ingratitude, not living up to expectations, shame, any act that was not in total compliance. Repeatedly, we hear about "nachas," the bringing of achievements in hopes of obtaining recognition from the parents.

Overprotection as a projection of the parents' sense of inadequacy, rather than a defect in the child, is explored. The double bind here is that frustration results when some of the parents are unable to express their satisfaction or pleasure. The effect this has upon the parents' marriages and the children's marriages is explored.

They talk of resentment at the loss of the function grandparents filled for their friends and their awareness that something had been different for them. This brings up a discussion of the lack of aging role models for their parents and themselves; that aging may be associated with the brutal deaths of the grandparents. We explored loss and the place of grief and mourning. Distortions and displacements resulting from incomplete mourning became apparent.

We discussed the development of natural parental reactions to the infant's dependency as it progresses on through autonomy with the concomitant conflicts. Especially noteworthy was how the children of survivors could be identified at times as the aggressors when asserting themselves, while at other times they are experienced and treated as the victim. The children of survivors often have heard their parents use expletives towards them which had been hurled at the parents in the camps.

Many other themes were touched upon. They include: fears of another Holocaust, feelings of shame and rage about the Holocaust, strong reactions to anti-semitism and the neo-Nazi groups, difficulties in establishing a Jewish identification or conversely Orthodox adherence, intense reactions about dating or marrying out of the faith, problems in establishing intimacy, feeling unique.

In a number of groups feelings have been described of alienation and isolation from other Americans, both Jewish and non-Jewish. Basic lack of trust, especially of non-Jews, was mentioned. Incidents of violence often related to authority and police problems, as well as in the military, have existed. There was evidence of suspicion of our motives; were we writing a book?

In the discussion groups time was spent on improving communication with parents, i.e., communication techniques such as active listening and role playing. We used the discussion of life cycle stages, pointing out that few of the parents have had role models for adolescent rebellion, adult emancipation, aging, retirement, and death.

Although we have no mechanism for contact with the parents at this time, there has been some feedback from several parents who have also experienced positive effects. One has related the improved attitude and genuine interest on the part of the son at Passover.

Recommendations for Treatment

Strongly to be suggested is the consideration of the homogeneous group for at least part of the individual's therapy. We are now using a longer-term, three-month, group-therapy approach, but have returned to an 8-10 session model. We would still caution against a long-term homogeneous group, although one is thriving in this community. Where further therapy is warranted, we feel a mixed group experience to be valuable and have embarked upon one recently. Half of the members of a young adult group are children of survivors. Individual and family therapy, as well as multifamily therapy, are valuable tools. Multigenerational groups should be utilized. These would permit issues of transference to be addressed, since two generations of unconscious material are in effect. We have not as yet staffed multi-family and multi-generational groups. There are indications that the passage of 30 years has brought changes in the survivor community. Some are asking for more open communication with their children and spouses. As a sign of this growing openness, survivor groups in this community are asserting their sense of enfranchisement. No longer do they accept the subtle pressures to deny their pain or to expose it only within the confines of survivor groups. Instead, they are endowing a chair in Holocaust studies at U.C.L.A., have been active in establishing the "Martyr's Memorial" within the Jewish Federation Council, and have been instrumental in Yeshiva University's founding of the Simon Wiesenthal Center. This indicates an overturning of the earlier denial and isolation imposed in North America, the result of which was much unfinished business within the family. Cautiously, these issues now may be addressed with selected families.

Thoughts on the Transmission of Pain

Matussek (1975), in his massive study using factor analysis of the consequences of internment in concentration camps, finds that those politically imprisoned, primarily non-Jews, are not suffering the extent of physical and emotional damage exhibited by Jewish survivors. It would be interesting to learn how many of these political survivors and their families have sought therapeutic intervention.

Despite this, we would expect that any person or group suffering prolonged life-threatening conditions would be candidates for outreach services, preventatively as well as remedially.

Richard Rabkin (1972) cites the French philosopher, Simone Weil, who suggests that the infliction of suffering from one victim to another may provide relief rather than remorse. Rabkin further discusses the means by which pain and evil, as social processes, are transmitted when the opportunity for full mourning is unavailable. This is supported in Goodman's (1978) dissertation.

However, this does not negate that strengths are also evidenced. If we agree that pain and suffering are transmittable one generation to the next, we must also accept the hypothesis that survival mechanisms, i.e., healthy suspiciousness, ambition, assertiveness, etc., are also passed on. In my extensive contacts with children of survivors this is a readily observable fact.

In conclusion, I have identified a major area of familial unfinished business. The responsibility to mitigate transferable damage to yet another generation lies, in part, with us as therapists and as individuals. The challenge, then, is to find channels for mourning and new methods to provide relief for both the victim and the descendants.

References

Axelrod, S. *Hospitalized children of holocaust survivors: Problems and dynamics.* Paper presented at the meeting of the American Psychiatric Association, New York, May 1978.
Becker, E. The pawnbroker: A study in basic psychology. In *Angel in armor: A post-Freudian perspective on the nature of man.* New York: Braziller, 1969.
Goodman, J. *The transmission of parental trauma: Second-generation effects of Nazi concentration camp survival.* Unpublished doctoral dissertation, California School of Professional Psychology, Fresno Campus, 1978.
Hoppe, K. The emotional reactions of psychiatrists when confronting survivors of persecution. In J. Lindon (Ed.), *Psychoanalytic forum.* New York: Science House, 1969.
International congress of child psychiatry and allied professions and the American association for child psychoanalysis, Jerusalem, August 1970.
Kanter, I. Social Psychiatry and the holocaust. *Journal of Psychology and Judaism,* 1976, *1*(1), 55-66.
Kestenberg, J. Introductory remarks. In E. Anthony & C. Koupernik (Eds.), *The child in his family: The impact of disease and death* (Vol. 2). New York: John Wiley & Sons, 1973.
Kinsler, F. The unfinished business of the family. Treatment of children of holocaust survivors: Thoughts and feelings of a therapist. In *The many dimensions of family practice: The proceedings of the North American symposium on family practice.* New York: Family Service Association of America, 1980.
Kohut, H. & Wolf, E. The disorders of the self and their treatment: An outline. *International Journal of Psycho-analysis,* 1978, *59*(4), 413-425.
Krystal, H. (Ed.). *Massive psychic trauma.* New York: International Universities Press, 1968.
Lifton, R. *Death in life: Survivors of Hiroshima.* New York: Simon & Shuster, 1976.
Matussek, P. [Internment in concentration camps and its consequences]. (D. & I. Jordan, trans.). New York & Berlin: Springer-Verlag, 1975.
Neiderland, G. Clinical observations on the "survivor syndrome." *International Journal of Psycho-Analysis, 1968, 49*(23), 313-315.
Pomerantz, B. The unfinished business of the family: Group treatment with children of survivors. In *The many dimensions of family practice: Proceedings of the North American symposium on family practice.* New York: Family Service Association of America, 1980.

Rabkin, R. Evil as a social process: The My Lai Massacre. In C. Sager & H. Caplan (Eds.), *Progress in group and family therapy.* New York: Bruner/Mazel, 1972.
Savran, B. & Fogelman, E. Therapeutic groups for children of holocaust survivors. *International Journal of Group Psychotherapy,* 1979, *29*(2), 211-235.
Sigal, J. Hypotheses and methodology in the study of families of holocaust survivors. In E. Anthony & C. Koupernik (Eds.), *The child in his family: The impact of disease and death* (Vol. 2). New York: John Wiley & Sons, 1973.
Sigal, J. Preoccupation and bonding. A report for the Congress of the World Federation for Mental Health. Vancouver, Canada, August 21, 1977.
Simos, B. *A time to grieve.* New York: Family Service Association of America, 1979.
Sonnenberg, S. *Children of survivors.* A report to the American Psychoanalytic Association and the Association for Child Psycho-analysis, New York City, December 1971.

A Proposal for Treating Adolescent Offspring of Holocaust Survivors

STANLEY SCHNEIDER has done his graduate work in psychology, social work and semitic languages at Yeshiva University. He is the Director of Summit Institute in Jerusalem, Israel and Adjunct Professor at the Wurzweiler School of Social Work, Yeshiva University. He has written and lectured extensively and is on the Editorial Advisory Panel of the International Journal of Therapeutic Communities. *This paper is adapted from a presentation to the American Association of Psychiatric Services for Children in Chicago in November, 1979.*

ABSTRACT: Over the past ten years a statistically significant population of adolescents of holocaust survivors has been diagnosed as suffering from "survivor syndrome." These offspring must be aided therapeutically and understood in light of recent clinical findings found among holocaust survivors. While ambulatory psychotherapy may be helpful to a certain segment of the affected population, residential treatment, and specifically, a Network of Psychiatric Services, may be the treatment of choice for others. Israel provides an excellent therapeutic milieu for these adolescents. Israel is specifically effective in engendering the attainment of positive identity goals for those who have difficulties in identity-confusion. Through identification the perpetuation of traumatization in generations yet unborn can be prevented.

And already you will be covered with skin and sinews and you will live, look, you will have your lives back, sit in the living room, read the evening paper. Here you are. Nothing is too late. (Pagis, 1976, p. 97)

The above selection, from the works of a 49 year old former concentration camp inmate, reflects the past and speaks cynically of the future. Is it really possible to cover over the past degrading, inhumane, traumatic experience? Can the lives of concentration camp prisoners really be returned to them? What about having future progeny? Pagis, who spent part of his adolescent years in a concentration camp, was deeply affected; his poetry reflects despair and anomie.

Journal of Psychology and Judaism, Vol. 6(1) Fall/Winter 1981
0700-9801/81/1500-0068$00.95© 1981 Human Sciences Press

This paper will deal with the topic of adolescent offspring of Holocaust survivors. While much has been published regarding the psychological problems of survivors of the Nazi Holocaust, there now is just beginning to emerge a literature on offspring of these survivors. Over the past ten years, mental health professionals have been treating disproportionate numbers of adolescents whose parents had been in concentration camps or were partisan fighters during the war.

An attempt will be made to portray the psychological composition of these survivor children. "Something" must have been transmitted to these children, consciously or unconsciously. Many of these children and adolescents suffer from an "identity crisis" — "Who am I?" While the "normal" adolescent goes through this questioning, the survivors' adolescent has to re-define an identity; the parents may have "lost" their identity.

Additionally, it will be shown how the Network of Psychiatric Services for Adolescents based in Jerusalem, Israel, as a venue, aids greatly in the "re-identification" process.

Survivors and Their Offspring: A Clinical Portrait

Survivors have been clinically diagnosed as suffering from the survivor syndrome with its concomitant depression and survivor guilt, and repressed aggression—depression and guilt because they survived, and repressed aggression for holding back their true feelings of anger, disgust and humiliation.

The survivor syndrome has two basic parts; a depressive component and a persecutory component. The former is typified by withdrawal, apathy and an intense, pervasive feeling of loneliness. There are also feelings of shame for having lowered oneself to self-denigrating, deprecating acts in order to survive. The persecutory component has the clinical manifestations of acute anxiety states and nightmares—some even suffer from paranoia.

The defense mechanism used by these victims has been termed "affect-lameness," "isolation of affect," "emotional anaesthesia," or, as Frankl terms it: "apathy, the blunting of the emotions and the feeling that one could not care anymore" (1963, p.35).

Dr. Jaffe of Shalvatta Psychiatric Hospital, Hod Hasharon, Israel, went even further. She concluded that:

> a bio-psychic irreversible alteration of the whole personality takes place which is caused by the impact of chronic somatic and psychic traumatisation, suggesting a pathologically altered constitution with newly acquired tendencies to neurotic reactions and behavior... a neurasthenic-like picture. (1963, p.93)

Werner Tuteur, in a follow-up study of 100 concentration camp survivors, 20 years later, found a surprising amount of EEG foci, indicating blunt head injuries. Also he found that many survivors show a 'burnt-out' appearance which must not be confused with that of a schizophrenic (1966).

What about the offspring of these survivors? It seems that the survivor syndrome pattern of functioning has been transmitted to these offspring. One finds depression, withdrawal, guilt, identity-confusion, anger and hostility, emotional impoverishment and a tremendous need for affection. These are precisely the clinical manifestations that are seen in the adult survivor.

Somehow, the parent has transmitted to the child this unfortunate legacy of the Holocaust. Studies have hypothesized that this may be due to the parents over-investing in their children, being extremely overprotective, or developing strong symbiotic ties between themselves and their children.

What is even more clear is that the "isolation of affect" mechanism has had an extremely deleterious effect on the emotional growth of the offspring. "The adolescent has not learned how to form appropriate relationships because his parents have been unable to convey to him appropriate, consistent, emotion-laden messages" (Schneider, 1978b, p. 581). Pagis describes this parental affection:

They love. They love not.
They love
a little. No.
A lot.
No.
Too much. (1976, p.116)

Some adolescents have even transformed their parents' survivor guilt into wishing their parents dead. "They have also transformed their parents' repressed aggressions into an acting-out phase of aggresivity (violence, suicidal acts, drugs, promiscuity and homosexuality)" (Schneider, 1978b, p.581).

In November, 1978, over 900 followers of the Reverend Jim Jones committed suicide in Jonestown, Guyana. Besides these victims, Representative Leo Ryan was murdered as he attempted to leave Jonestown. A 32 year old man, Laurence Layton, was charged with the murder. Laurence Layton's mother had escaped from Nazi Germany in 1938. Her parents were rounded-up with other Jews and herded into a train destined for the death camps. They tried committing suicide by swallowing poison capsules, but the pills didn't work. The couple was removed unconscious from the train and they eventually escaped to the United States. Just a coincidence?

Identity Formation and Holocaust Offspring

Identity formation is a constantly evolving process which takes into account the synthesis of the individual and society. The roots of this development are in earliest childhood, and the natural end is in the culmination of the adolescent stage.

The developing of an identity allows the person to recognize the self and to feel recognized. This "inner" and "outer" identity is the end result of the bridge between childhood and adolescence. "The adolescent search for a new and yet a reliable identity can perhaps best be seen in the persistent endeavor to define, to over-define and to redefine oneself and each other in often ruthless comparison" (Erikson, 1964, p.92).

Erikson feels that ego-identity represents the mediation between the internal mechanism operating in the adolescent and the social reality, i.e., environment. When difficulties arise the term "identity confusion" may be utilized (1974).

To the adolescent of Holocaust survivors, major problems emerge in the area of identity formation, mediation and identity confusion. Do these adolescents identify as Jews? Do they see a conflict between being Jewish and being an American? Do they relate being Jewish as being one of the "untermenschin" and therefore the message conveyed to the offspring is that of being the victim? Or is there a reaction-formation whereby the parents transmit their guilt about their Jewishness to defend against the rage at having been victimized for being Jewish? Do Holocaust survivors who have immigrated to Israel transmit less pathological messages to their children?

Erikson, in writing about identity, stated that Freud once linked his connection to the Jewish people by speaking of an "inner identity." Erikson felt that this exclusiveness was not based on race or religion. Rather it was "an individual's link with the unique values, fostered by a unique history, of his people" (1959, p.102).

The sense of peoplehood and community (in addition to family) is crucial to the development and enhancement of an adolescent's self-image, self-esteem and feeling of belonging. "Ethnicity is a group's collective history, which children inherit from their parents and, in turn, pass on to their offspring" (Giordano, 1976, p.3). When Holocaust survivors immigrated to countries other than Israel, they had to integrate into a foreign society and culture. Oft times conflicts arose: dual allegiance, anti-semitism, a need to blend-in and not be different. Those who immigrated to Israel seem to have fared better. Newman writes:

> When they arrived, Israel was fighting for its existence and every individual was valued. Some went directly from their port of entry to the battlefields of the 1948 war. (1979, p.49)

Israel respects the value of each individual to contribute to its society, taking into account all individual differences. Residents of Israel are also fighting for a goal, and in the wars, are fighting for their very existence. However, the most important ingredient is the fact that the establishment of a Jewish State, out of the ashes of 6,000,000 Jews, gives meaning to the holocaust and "defeats the Nazi attempt at genocide" (Newman, 1979, p.49).

Winnick (1967) feels that while the new State of Israel could not provide Holocaust survivors with a role (state) model to emulate and adapt to, nonetheless, this served as a tremendous advantage. These new immigrants were not forced to give up their former way of life, their social values, customs and symbols. They were now a major force in the new social order that was being created. They had a say in the governing of their own individual lives *plus* the added responsibility of a collective—the "Yishuv." This was very important to these survivors, many of whom had lost their families.

Israel provided a good venue for being better able to work through the traumatic effects of the Holocaust. Put differently, being Jewish in a Jewish State took the defensiveness away from the Jewishness. As an aside, there is another component besides the Jewish State—that is, the notion of the small group, or community. Eitinger did a study in 1975, where he followed-up Jewish and non-Jewish Norwegian survivors of the concentration camps, 30 years later. He found that the Jews managed better after their experiences than did the non-Jewish Norwegians. "It is concluded that the close knit milieu and the active acceptance and help of the small Jewish community in Norway have contributed to this" (Eitinger, 1975, p. 321).

In a study, after the Six Day War, of attitudes of American and Israeli Jewish youth towards victims of the Holocaust, Klein and Last (1967) found that knowledge was higher in the Israeli group and that Israeli children reflected a greater sense of identification with the problems of the continuity of the Jewish people and the dangers of annihiliation. The Six Day War re-awakened in many the threat of another Holocaust. Yet, in the end, it pulled-together the entire country, in ways reminiscent of the 1948 War of Independence. Survival, and the threat of its being taken away, allows aggression to be turned against a common enemy. "The feelings of humiliation, degradation and helplessness...can be corrected through victory"(Klein, 1967, p.96).

Kestenberg also felt that "participation in liberating wars such as World War II or Israeli Wars...allowed for the re-working of attitudes towards death and survival." This is considered to be "a reparation or undoing of genocide" (1972, p.321).

What about child-rearing? Did the Holocaust survivor have to "undo" in order to be a "normal" parent? Psychoanalytically, the survivor, unless able to find meaning in life and re-build psychic structure, cannot complete the mourning for family and self. Unless the survivor can re-build his/her image, children will not respect the survivor, who in turn will not be able to relate emotionally to them.

Newman (1979) feels that Israeli Society makes it easier for survivors to parent; whether it is on a kibbutz or in the city. Besides an extensive network of day care and child care clinics, there are certain religious, cultural and social milestones that aid separation, individuation and cultural identification. Confirmation ceremonies (Bar Mitzvah, Bat Mitzvah) are acceptable practices even among the most irreligious. Jewish Holidays, traditions and practices are studied in even the state-run, non-religious schools. Every child's entering the army at age 18 makes patriotism a viable and real value. Days of national mourning for the victims of the Holocaust and for those who fell in Israel's Wars makes for a collective remembrance.

Thus it is clear that Israeli society can help add more meaning to life and aid in re-defining a "lost" or damaged identity. An adolescent who is having emotional problems typical to survivors' offspring cannot camouflage himself in his own society. Israel can greatly aid the process. The adolescent finds more meaning and outlets for expression in Israel. Even moving from New York to California will not remove this adolescent's "stigma," for the adolescent will be recognized wherever he/she goes. In Israel, he/she stands another chance and has the opportunity to try again. The country needs everyone and the adolescent feels it, and is part of the cultural and national identification process. It is one's own country and one now has an investment to make.

Treatment for Adolescent Offspring of Holocaust Survivors

While some clinicians wonder whether there is a specificity in the emotional make-up of survivors' children, there is no question that there are disproportionate numbers of these children seeking treatment. The first problem, then, seems to be recognition of the problem and its more precise identification. When the patient and problem are identified, then treatment can commence.

It may be interesting to note that a study (Schneider, 1978a) was done on attitudes towards death in adolescent offspring of Holocaust survivors in order to see if an at-risk population could be identified before problems erupted. It was found that on the Thematic Apperception Test (TAT), several cards loaded heavy with a population of survivors' children. So from a purely preventative vantage point, there may be the possibility of an early-warning system in testing an at-risk population.

One may say, that any form of treatment for this population group (approach and/or modality) may be appropriate. However, for some adolescents, psychotherapy on an ambulatory basis may not be sufficient. A temporary "parentectomy" (Schneider, 1978 a) may be necessary because of the pathological nexus in the parent-child interaction and relationship. In this case, a therapeutic approach that is both nurturant and firm and is able to set needed limits is essential in order to provide restitution for the affectional deprivation and to aid in re-defining an identity.

If ambulatory treatment is ruled out as being insufficient, and, on the other extreme, psychiatric hospitalization is ruled out as being unnecessary or too confining, then residential treatment may be the treatment of choice.

Summit Institute in Israel began in September of 1973, as a residential treatment center for adolescents. Three years later when it began working with a multicultural population (Americans and Israelis), it was realized that *just* residential treatment was not enough. What was needed in working with emotionally disturbed adolescents, and specifically survivors' adolescents, was a Network of Psychiatric Services of Adolescents. With a network a wider variety of treatment services can be offered. This allows for more appropriate disposition and better treatment. In addition, an increase in responsibility and stability in the client population is met with a decrease in staffing and intensity of treatment.

It has been found that in adolescent offspring of Holocaust survivors, if the goal is to help correct the emotional past, continuity of care and continuation with the same therapist is essential. A Network of Services with a network staff that follows the adolescent through the treatment process, from the moment of referral until discharge from whatever is the last facility, is the best way to help disturbed adolescents.

Institute staff serves as the centralized body coordinating treatment/education/vocation and recreation services. In the *residential treatment center,*the focus is on a high student-staff ratio (1:1) in order to facilitate the treatment process, re-work through relationships and re-define an identity. The average client population here is 20-25.

The next step up is on to the *"high-expectations" half-way house.* Here 5-7 students live together in a house with limited staff coverage. Here the emphasis is on independence and being able to work/study and live "on the outside."

The next step is the *transitional home apartment*. These apartments are for those who are ready to begin living independently without live-in staff supervision. The emphasis here is on termination.

There is another type of half-way house: the *"nurturing" half-way house*. The focus here is on more long-term care, with the emphasis in treatment being on the illness of the student rather than on health. A student may begin in this type of half-way house, or may end up there if the other parts of the system do not help to foster change.

The last part of the Network is the *out-patient department*. Here students can be followed by the *same* therapist while living at home with their families, in foster families, or on their own.

For those adolescents in crisis, there is an affiliation with a local *psychiatric hospital* where they can be hospitalized for short periods (1-2 weeks). They then return to the Network program.

Additionally, there is an *educational/vocational center*, in a separate building, that has overall responsibility for providing education and job training to all parts of the Network.

Our Network of Psychiatric Services at Summit creates structure with continuity. This enables us to treat a population that requires a re-structuring of personality and aids in the re-identification process. We have found, over the past seven and a half years the program has been in existence, that to the American adolescent of Holocaust survivors, an extended period in Israel (within a properly structured therapeutic environment) is one of the most important treatment tools in recovery and rehabilitation. Here the adolescent is provided with a feeling of Jewish identification in a positive way. He is given the opportunity of experiencing participation in "front line" service and close identification with those (in Israel) who have recovered from similar trauma in a most dynamic and meaningful way.

Our model "provides 'treatment through process' with growth experiences in an experiential manner; total community (milieu) involvement within a group framework. An individualized treatment plan is proposed per student with ego-supporting modalities (ecucational/vocational/recreational)" (Schneider, 1978a, p.5).

The basic elements of the program are the following:

Principle	Construct
1. Structure	Experiential
a. "time"	
b. program	
c. therapeutic involvement	
2. Responsibility	Relationships
a. individual to self and group	

b. group to individual and
group
3. Control and Substitution   Treatment with
  a. control of acting-out,   Ego-Supporting
  deviant behavior   Modalities
  b. substitution of socially
  acceptable behavior

Through this highly structured program with a major thrust on re-
identification, we are able to help adolescents and young adults with
life-adjustment difficulties.

It has been found that treatment of adolescent offspring of
Holocaust survivors in the Network of Psychiatric Services provides
them with the close, nurturant and firm response that is needed in
order to "turn them around." Kestenberg uses the term
"rehabilitative restitution" (1972, p. 322).

References

Eitinger, L. Jewish concentration camp survivors in Norway. *Israel Annals of Psychiatry and Related Disciplines*, 1975, *13*(4), 321-334.
Erikson, E. *Identity and the life cycle.* New York: International Universities Press, 1959
Erikson, E. *Insight and responsibility.* New York: W. W. Norton, 1964.
Erikson, E. *Identity: Youth and crisis.* London: Faber and Faber, 1974.
Frankl, V. *Man's search for meaning: An introduction to logotherapy.* New York: Washington Square Press, 1963.
Giordano, J. Group identity and mental health: Overview. *International Journal of Mental Health*, 1976, *5*(2), 3-147.
Jaffe, R. Symposium on psychological disorders among holocaust survivors—Israel Psychoanalytic Society, July, 1966. *Israel Annals of Psychiatry and Related Disciplines*, 1967, *5*(1), 93.
Kestenberg, J. Psychoanalytic contributions to the problem of children of survivors from Nazi persecution. *Israel Annals of Psychiatry and Related Disciplines, 1972, 10*(4), 311-325.
Klein, H. Symposium on psychological disorders among holocaust survivors—Israel Psychoanalytic Society, July, 1966. *Israel Annals of Psychiatry and Related Disciplines, 1967, 5*(1), 91-100.
Klein, H. & Last. U. Cognitive and emotional aspects of the attitudes of American and Israeli Jewish youth towards the victims of the holocaust. *Israel Annals of Psychiatry and Related Disciplines,* 1967, *12*(2), 111-131.
Newman, L. Emotional disturbance in children of holocaust survivors. *Social Casework*, 1979, *60*(1), 43-50.
Pagis, D. *Selected poems.* Middlesex, England: Penguin Books, 1976.
Schneider, S. A model for an alternative educational/treatment program for adolescents.*Israel Annals of Psychiatry and Related Disciplines,*1978, *16*(1), 1-20. (a)
Schneider, S. Attitudes towards death in adolescent offspring of holocaust survivors. *Adolescence*, 1978,*13*(52), 575-584. (b)
Tuteur, W. One hundred concentration camp survivors—Twenty years later.*Israel Annals of Psychiatry and Related Disciplines*, 1966, *4*(1), 78-90.
Winnik, H. Further comments concerning problems of late psychopathological effects of Nazi-persecution and their therapy. *Israel Annals of Psychiatry and Related Disciplines,*1967, *5*(1), 1-16.